Persian Tea

Persian Tea

Jasmine Lawi

Dedication

I remember my grandmother praying that I get married one day. I was only nine years old. She loved to dance at weddings, and I believed that she was the happiest woman in the world.

Her red nail polish always matched her red lipstick, and I cherished holding her soft hands. She loved to tell jokes that were entailed with kisses and flirty innuendos. My grandmother relished playing a card game of Rummy especially because her memory was razor-sharp. Indeed, her favorite place in the world was Las Vegas.

She loved to tell stories and spill wisdom over Persian tea.

One precious moment, she joined her index and middle fingers to mimic a cigarette. After she blew "smoke," she imparted serious advice. She urged, "Take many trips to Las Vegas with your husband. Always sit beside him at the Poker table. Like a sultry temptress, hold a cigarette in one hand and a cocktail in the other." Afterward, she sipped her hot tea like a martini, and pouted her cherry-colored lips as she gently snuggled against the sofa's soft pillow to *really* show me how it's done.

One day, my grandmother asked my father to buy her a cellphone because she was very popular. Thereafter, her ringtone rang incessantly. Likewise, she called me on many evenings. Concerned, I asked, "Where are you?" She pressed her cellphone against her cherry-colored lips and said, "I'm home." Her tone was predictably matter of fact despite her operative landline.

With her iron will and tender heart, she raised three successful doctors and had 14 wonderful grandchildren.

My grandmother always told me, "You're my favorite," and I had a funny inkling that I wasn't the only one. The last time that we had met for tea, she was resting in bed and twirling her hands in the air like a beautiful dancing butterfly.

I whispered to her, "Promise to call me in my dreams," and from time to time, she does.

I love you.

For me, "soulmate" surpasses romance. A "soulmate" can also be a best friend, mentor, or relative. This was confirmed to me when I read its literal definition: "A person ideally suited to another, as a close friend or romantic partner."

More so, my understanding of reincarnation under *Kaballah* (Jewish Mysticism) is that souls of family members may travel together in past and future lives. A brother and sister in one life may be a father and daughter in another.

I believe that my Father is a soulmate of mine.

Dad, as a child, I never let you out of my sight. I felt best when I was near you, after all, we are soulmates. It's no coincidence that your actions effortlessly led me to my husband-my romantic *besheret* ("soulmate" in Hebrew).

Mom, although Dad's instincts and actions opened the door for me to live in Israel and place me in physical and spiritual proximity to my future husband, it was your love that encouraged me to shoot for the stars.

Mom and Dad, I only wish that every reader will grasp the level of sacrifice and selfless devotion that you have exhibited for me and my two adoring brothers. You were newlyweds and new parents amidst the chaos of the Iranian Revolution. Yet, you saved our family and courageously set voyage to a new country, a new language, and a new culture in America.

You embarked on this enormous challenge with grace, faith in God, determination, and most of all love.

Dad, with all of your heart and will, you returned to university and obtained your Dental license in New York State and in California. You are amazingly wise and brave. This is evident by the fact that along with your Dental practice, you have simultaneously built a real estate enterprise. I'm so proud of you.

You have a giant heart, and because of that I was blessed with a beautiful life. You taught me to ski, swim, and ride a bike. Dad, like fine wine, you only improve with age.

I believe that behind every great man is an incredible woman.

Mom, you are the reason for Dad's success and happiness. Your relentless dedication and belief in him encouraged Dad to pursue his Dental license in America. With patience and grace, you translated all of his studies to Farsi and then translated it back to English so that he would grasp everything in its entirety.

In New York, singlehandedly, you took us out for endless hours to grant Dad quiet study time. Even to this day, you lovingly prepare Dad freshly squeezed orange juice and a gourmet lunch so that he has the energy to work hard.

Mom and Dad, the boundaries are endless to your sacrifice for our family.

I love you.

My Dearest Husband,

You are the reason that I write. One day, you said to me, "You are a talented writer." These simple words embarked me on a voyage that I never dreamed.

While preparing for our wedding, Cantor Benjamin asked several questions, including what made me fall in love with you. I answered, "Everything!"

You are incredibly sexy, brave, confident, resilient, centered, wise beyond your years, intuitive, enlightened in so many ways, blessed, and of course irresistibly charming.

Your beautiful qualities are validated to me every single day.

Your inner peace. Your gratitude. Your touch. Your scent. Your unconditional love.

You are my mentor and philosopher. You are kind and gentle, yet strong and powerful. You are incredibly patient and the best kisser. I love your desire for excitement and adventure.

Your bravery in the face adversity is my rock.

You are my love, my strength, my handsome husband, and my best friend. Above all, you are our daughter's protector.

You see my darling, your relentless loyalty reflects the husband and father that you have become. To say that we are in good hands is without a doubt an understatement.

I love you.

Table of Contents

Table of Contents

Preface

We take a walk in a field of dreams. The hay is high, and the sun is strikingly bold. We saunter on hand in hand. I have so much to tell, and you are eager to listen. I walk you through this voyage transcending time and space.

The journey begins in 1979 when the Islamic Revolution struck Iran. It was the terrifying "shot heard around the world." Shortly after, my family courageously left Iran for America.

These stories unraveled were kept secret until now. No longer shackled by Revolutionary dogmas and immigrant insecurity, our voices grew loud and strong. Even if the conundrums and punchlines that we utter dreadfully linger in a Persian accent.

The stories you will read are vignettes of an enchanted life engulfed in sheer luck, wild adventures, colossal mishaps, spellbinding romance, ferocious death, and "golden nuggets" elicited from dare I say, Devils.

So together, I invite you to close your eyes and enjoy the reverie.

Jasmine

Persian Tea

Amnesia

I was born on August 1, 1977, in Tehran, Iran. Two years later, the Iranian Revolution ("the Revolution") set the country ablaze.

On January 16, 1979, Shah Mohammad Reza Pahlavi ("the Shah") ("Shah" is "King" in Farsi) was overthrown and replaced with the Islamic Republic, under the Ayatollah Ruhollah Khomeini.

My parents and many Iranian Jews alike feared religious persecution and a Holocaust.

In June 1979, my parents took a Swissair flight to London and said their last goodbye to their once beloved country. I was nearly two years old, and my brother Ezra was five months old.

After two weeks in London, we left for Israel. In October 1979, after three months in Israel, we immigrated to America penniless.

I vaguely remember my childhood. The car that we drove. My bedroom. Playing tag. My first-grade teacher.

Yet, I recall some defining moments in my life.

It was December 1979, I was two years old, and my brother was one. We lived in the rat-infested slums of Queens, New York. Every day, we bundled up for pre-school, and my mom pushed our stroller through the borough's icy pavements.

For many years, she trekked in blizzards and snow because we could not afford a car. I saw first-hand, my parents' unyielding sacrifice and devotion.

In 1982, at the age of five, my family and I fled the arctic freeze of New York, and we arrived in sunny California.

I was seven years old, and I cut the lunch line to stand next to a cute boy. I even held his hand. In that tender moment, I discovered my bravery to pursue all of my dreams and desires wholeheartedly.

On my eighth Birthday, I bid farewell to our tiny apartment. On our way to our new and big home, we drove through Wilshire Boulevard in Los Angeles. I made sure to point out every building that I had once lived in, and there were many!

Just to name a few (and don't be fooled by their "fancy" names), we lived at the Westwood Versailles. Then, the Wilshire Picasso. From there, the Pink Lady Hotel. After that, the Royal Estina.

We moved because we got evicted, and we got evicted because we were immigrants.

I neatly stowed this in life's treasure chest of silver linings. Sometimes, life is unfair, and people can be mean. Even so, in 1985 we bought our home and stayed forever.

Tomorrow Never Dies

My son Ezra was born in Tehran, Iran, on January 1, 1979, amid mayhem and revolution.

I disobeyed the military curfew and gallantly drove at night to Shahram Hospital. I *had* to get my wife, Firoozeh, and new baby home.

I owned an olive green BMW sedan. For its time, it was chic and sexy. I felt like James Bond 007.

Angry teenagers and veiled women threw stones at the Shah's army. I imagined James Bond's car chase in *Goldfinger*. My wheels skid over gravel and potholes. I made smooth, fast turns into alleyways and roundabouts. My "Bondmobile" dodged gunshots, fire, tear gas, and molotov cocktails. I calculated that I was a fair target for the mob and the army!

Amidst the smokey-faced radicals, I locked eyes with Reza. He was my friend and classmate.

My dear Tehran turned to ashes. Iranian confidantes, I called *"baradar"* ("brother" in Farsi) chanted *"Mag bar Amrika! Mag bar Eesrael!"* ("Death to America! Death to Israel!" in Farsi).

Young men flung tree branches at Shahram Hospital, and piles of wood and rubbish forged a makeshift barricade. I crusaded against heaping stacks of reddish brown timber and finally made headways toward the glass door.

Green leaves with yellowish hues and ripped sheets of papers that were infused with bold propaganda floated inside.

Shahram Hospital became a defenseless enclave that was trapped inside the mean streets of Tehran. Even the most devout simpleton knew that the rebels had planned to torch fire and anarchy to this elusive safe haven.

Only one day after giving birth, my beautiful and courageous wife mustered her strength to leave. My left arm clutched Ezra, and my right locked arms with Firoozeh. Like the undefeated and zealous armies of Cyrus the Great, we diligently marched through the ugly trenches of shattered glass, shrapnel, and human hysteria.

I made sure that Firoozeh reclined with Ezra in the back seat. This way, they remained "bulletproof." I estimated, if I got shot, Jasmine and Ezra still had Firoozeh. Thus, in a similar fashion to my arrival, I stepped on the gas and sped off! I raised an arrogant brow as I glanced at my rearview. Through the mirror's lens, I smirked at the winding tire tracks that were left behind to fend for themselves like dust to the wind.

Our neighbor, Mrs. Shamshiri, greeted us and then boldly stated, "All *our* sons are dying. Yet, you brought yours home."

Mrs. Shamshiri was nearly recognizable. Usually adorned in emeralds and shiny lipstick, she donned a silk headscarf, oversized black-tinted sunglasses, and nude lips.

Despite Mrs. Shamshiri's aggressive attempt to conceal her allure, her porcelain like skin elegantly shimmered beneath the moonlight, and that was my final clue to the uncanny woman that was seen outside of my home.

Sixteen days after my son was born, the Shah and his family left Iran for Egypt. I watched his exile on television.

His thin lips clamped in unwilling surrender. His teary eyes screamed "defeat!" His gaze reflected big misery and sorrow.

In the streets, Iranians rejoiced and chanted, *"Shah farori shodeh!"* ("Shah was scared and ran away!" in Farsi).

If Shakespeare was alive then, he would contend that the Shah's legacy was a tragedy greater than his own *King Lear*. My beloved Shah was banished from his Kingdom. *Where did that leave me?* As a Jew, I feared for my life.

On May 8, 1979, the Islamic Republic ("the Islamic Regime") convicted Habib Elghanian, a prominent Iranian Jewish businessman, of Zionism. One day later, he was executed by firing squad.

That instant, Firoozeh and I made a resolute decision to flee. Yet, first things first, we had to make sure that Firoozeh's father left Iran alive.

All the King's Men

Utopia

Then and now, I love my father-in-law like I did my late father, God bless his soul.

Like King Arthur's Round Table, the Shah met with his most trusted and wealthy "Knights." Amongst them sat my father-in-law, *Baba jan,* and the likes of Habib Elghanian. ("Baba jan" means "Dear father" in Farsi.) Baba jan exported Iranian dried fruits to Russia and throughout Europe.

In Tehran, the Knights met at the *Ohtageh Asnat* ("Room of the Business") inside the Ministry of Business. It was there that they gave the Shah economic reports for their trades and commerce.

Baba Jan's destiny to sit with the Shah at his Round Table did not unfold overnight. His voyage began in a beautiful city tucked away inside the fertile terrain of Iran's Azerbaijan Province ("Iranian Azerbaijan") by the name of Urmia.

Like Father, Like Son

Baba jan was born in Urmia in 1928. From a very young age, he was ambitious.

In the 1930's, Reza Shah Pahlavi (the Shah's father) visited Urmia. In his honor, people sacrificed precious livestock and painted the streets with colorful bright lights.

Gifted musicians played their *dombaks,* and percussion sound waves travelled while children danced to the beat of the folklore music. ("Dombak" is a goblet shaped, wooden drum.)

Reza Shah became captivated by Urmia's majestic beauty. So much so, that he named it Rezaiyeh after himself. (After the Revolution, the Islamic Regime changed the name back to Urmia.)

Urmia's rich soil and lush agriculture yielded a wealth of fruit fit for a King, especially its juicy apples and succulent grapes. There, Baba jan, his father, and two brothers produced dried fruit, primarily raisins.

The Roaring 20's

It wasn't always Utopia.

There was a period of time in which Russia ruled the Soviet Republic of Azerbaijan bordering Iranian Azerbaijan, and Russia desired power over the Iranian Provinces.

Russian tanks and brazen, blue-eyed commandos patrolled hidden corners and blind spots inside Iranian Azerbaijan. Between seasons, the Red Army and the Persian Army engaged in duels, and Iran was invincible.

Natives of Urmia waltzed beside the shadows of the Russian army in order to survive the rocky times. For example, young women were betrothed to Russian soldiers, and ambitious men bridged Russian connections.

Before Baba jan worked with his father, he was 17 years old and sold textiles in Urmia. His storefront stood like a speckle on the street of Maydoon Shahrpoor.

By his 19th birthday, he was a major textile dealer in Urmia, and demand had surpassed his medley of supplies that were kept neat inside his tiny parlor. Artisans and seamstresses loyal to Baba jan had a penchant for more, and he had to satiate their ravenous appetites.

The City of Tabriz was the Mecca of the fabric industry inside Iranian Azerbaijan, and it produced treasures of silk, wool, and cotton. Baba jan gathered intelligence and found the key to unlocking his treasure chest.

A peculiar, brown-eyed Russian chauffeur ("the Russian") crept across the dark night inside his military jeep. The exotic vehicle belonged to his commandant, and it was the only car that was inside Urmia. A scarce few knew that he travelled at midnight to transfer top-secret intelligence to Russian headquarters that were buried deep inside the grim caves of Tabriz, which seven centuries ago were vibrant villages carved from stone.

One night, a shy headlight blinked twice, and that was Baba jan's cue to dive into the jeep. Inside, he removed his cap and shook hands with a businessman ("the Businessman") who was disguised in a mustache. The trio journeyed across abandoned one-way roads and tucked away passageways.

That night was *supposed* to be like every other night.

The proceeded to trek by stick shift with a clutch, behaving rusty on all surfaces, to reach the desolate shipyard that was cast in the scary outskirts of Urmia. From there, Baba jan sought voyage to Sharabchooneh (a small town), and upon his arrival, he boarded a train with a quick stop in Tabriz.

Sleepy-eyed gypsy children anticipating Baba jan while dreaming fairytales of faraway lands that harvest yields of gold were roused from their fantasies when they heard his ship dock.

They huddled on the railway's platform for the sake of their hungry stomachs, empty pockets, and tiny hands full of treats! Baba jan savored their sugared round bread, mouthwatering sour plums, and salty black licorice. With a penchant for being magnanimous, he was their chief patron, and the children's pockets were not so empty anymore.

That foggy night, when the Russian made a sudden detour into the bleak desert valley, Baba jan knew that he would miss his train *and* delicacies.

Grains of sand accumulated into the air when the Russian spun donuts like a maniac into the dry soil to ignite fear down to their bones. He roared an evil laugh before he slammed his foot on the brake to turn his head about. Right then, Baba jan and the Businessman stared evil dead in the face.

When the Russian squinted his brown eyes while he pointed his pistol, they turned red like a demon's eyes. The Russian's actions truly spoke louder than words, but he spoke anyways when he loudly whispered, *"De-ngi! De-ngi!"* ("Money! Money!" in Russian).

With his pistol, he motioned them to remove the money inside their coats. Even so, droplets of sweat slipped down the Russian's face, and his handgun began to shake. Baba jan had 50 *Tomans* (Iranian currency) inside his pocket, but the Businessman had more.

The Russian licked his index finger to help count his loot, and the men remained still while time was fleeing against their favor.

Through the voice of the desert wind howls, Baba jan heard his fate be told. The air was colder than he had imagined, and with his hat left inside the jeep, he used his pockets to keep his hands warm.

Before they heard the Russian cock his pistol, he ordered the men to turn their backs.

They didn't see the Russian speed off. Only when the taillights drifted away in the far distance, leaving them alone in pitch darkness, did they believe that they were scot free!

Baba jan's cold hands patted the front sides of his body in the same manner that one repeats after he's dogged a real-life bullet. But in fact, he was verifying that his stash of cash hidden underneath his shirt in a sewn sack, that was tied around his waist like a belt, remained intact.

The fog disappeared when the moon lit up the sky, and they followed the constellation of the stars to find their way home.

Alas, Baba jan and his 1,500 Tomans arrived home safely. Thereafter, he travelled to Tabriz only in daylight, and the Russian vanished like a ghost.

On his way home, the desert wind howls spoke softly to Baba jan, and his fate for good fortune and longevity was sealed that frightfully lucky night.

Peace, Love, and the 60's

In 1952, Baba jan's father left this world. The three brothers stayed united and inherited the "throne." Bounteous seeds for Baba jan's dried fruit empire were planted, and he was only 24 years old.

One decade and a half later, Baba jan established seven factories that stretched across Iran's landscape. Moreover, he lead 1,400 skilled men and women. His fleet was ambitious for anyone, especially for a Jew inside an Islamic country.

Baba jan's cavalry feared God, valued integrity, and navigated through a moral compass. Like eclectic patterns in an undivided mosaic, Muslims, Christians, Baha'is, and Jews worked together in harmony, and the factories became a melting pot of ancient Persian and Turkish languages.

Baba jan *also* spoke a "secret" Jewish language named *Lishan Didan*, which literally means "Our Language." Lishan Didan is a Jewish dialect of Aramaic and was spoken by the Jews of Urmia.

Despite differences in Gods, prophets, and old-age linguistics, Baba jan upheld his allegiance to his devoted company men and women, and they did so in return.

"I Have a Dream"

In 1960, in Rezaiyeh, Baba jan met the Shah inside the *Ostendari*. ("Ostendari" means the "Governor's grand chambers" in Farsi.) Like most of his royal portraits, the Shah arrived dressed in military uniform.

A tiny circle of Assyrian, Armenian, Muslim, and only three Jewish businessmen were bequeathed his royal invitation.

Back then, Turkey and Greece were the supreme exporters of dried fruit, and Baba jan aspired for Iran to compete globally. The Shah shared this dream.

After the Ostendari, the Shah opened the gateways to expand Iran's domestic and international dried fruit trade. For example, he pledged low interest bank loans and reduced train fares. For this reason, Iran's dried fruit trade boomed triumphantly.

Spring Fever

In 1963, Baba jan and Mama jan moved to Shemiran, Tehran and lived close to the Shah's residence-The Niavaran Palace ("the Palace"). The square, stone-faced Palace sat on a large green garden surrounded by blooming rose beds.

The Shah loved to take strolls through its tree-studded lawns and race his sports cars along its smooth roads. An accomplished aviator, he daringly flew his blue and white helicopter to and from the Palace as well.

In March 1968, the Shah invited Iran's esteemed businessmen and their wives to celebrate *Nowruz*. ("Nowruz" is the Persian New Year.) Mama jan and Baba jan entered the palatial estate through the ornate iron gates of the Palace.

Inside, the Palace floors were made of black granite stones that sparkled from dusk until dawn. Silk Persian carpets gracefully led the way into the vast central foyer. The sliding aluminum ceiling, three-stories high above the foyer, dramatically opened in the middle.

French tapestries gifted by Charles de Gaulle and Czech chandeliers hung stoic and high. The scent of springtime wafted through the air. It was a romantic era reminiscent of modernity and opulence.

It's the 70's Baby

In 1971, the Shah hosted a royal ball inside the Shahyad Tower ("the Tower"). The Tower was *specially* built to mark the 2,500 Year Celebration of the Persian Empire. A galaxy of Kings and their Queens, Presidents and Prime Ministers, Courtiers and Viceroys, and affluent businessmen were his Majesty's guests.

At a height of 148 feet, the inverted Y-shaped Tower stood watchful and courageous. Just like the peacock, a symbol of Persian monarchy, when he spreads his beautiful plumage far and wide.

The Tower is entirely clad with 8,000 blocks of precious white marble, mined from the icy mountains of Isfahan.

In the gardens, water soared from fountains like liquid fireworks, and floodlights surrounding the Tower were dimly lit. Mama jan and Baba jan entered the Tower through its main doors, which were made of granite specially excavated from the rocky mountains of Hamadan and weighed 7,000 tons.

Inside the main hall, the walls were draped in black marble, and enormous chandeliers, made of Bohemian crystals, lit up the darkness.

At the center, the Cylinder of Cyrus the Great rested on a tall stand, and adjacent was a gold plate from Persepolis (ancient capital of the Persian Empire) that was inscribed by Xeres (ancient Persian King). It read: "I built this building and I will build many better ones in the future."

Nearby, a bronze statue of Reza Shah looking austere greeted his guests.

One hand-weaved rug with intricate details of gallant Persian kingdoms and astute giant lions as defenders of the throne covered the *entire* flooring, and 500 blue velvety chairs with oyster-shaped backrests patiently waited for their guests.

Different shapes and hues of gemstones sparkled on women's ears and décolletés. Their hair was uncovered, and glamorous updos like the French Twist and Bouffant competed for the spotlight.

The colors of the rainbow radiated that night through women's gowns made of silk and embellished with gold and silver threading. Mama jan wore her gold necklace with a pink satin gown and chiffon poncho.

The Shah dressed in gala, and his chest was adorned with medallions. Men wore tuxedos with tailcoats, and Heads of State wore sashes over their right shoulders as a symbol of their power.

Smooth classical music played in the background to the sound of Schubert and Mozart, and while the orchestra performed, waiters in white dinner jackets served black caviar that was collected from sturgeons of the Caspian Sea on sterling silver trays. Thousands of bottles of French champagne imported from Paris to Tehran popped open one after the next and were poured in Baccarat crystal flutes.

In his speech, the Shah spoke strongly and paid tribute to Iran's businessmen. His speech was bereft of words like murder, war, and hate. Queen Farrah (the Shah's wife) listened steadfastly as she stayed by his side.

By happenstance, Mama jan sat side-by-side with the Queen of Jordan. Back then, Israel and Jordan were sworn enemies. Little did the Empress know that she sat beside a Jew that princely night.

1979

Baba jan was, and remains tall and powerfully built. He's armed with broad shoulders, large hands, and a deep strong voice. Even so, he smiles with his soft blue eyes and loves with his kind, big heart. Just like his strength and devotion, Baba jan's humility remains steadfast.

In 1979, Baba jan swiftly left Iran for Switzerland with my help.

Having seized power, the Islamic Regime immediately blacklisted the Shah's Knights, Jews *and* Muslims alike.

Baba jan departed with one small suitcase in his hand, leaving his heart and giant business deeply entrenched inside Iran.

Three hours later, the *Sepah* (Islamic Revolutionary Guard) came to search for him inside his home. Firoozeh and I were neighbors with her parents. Thus, it was not a coincidence that we were there.

They demanded to know where he was. I told them the truth. "I don't know." He was safe somewhere in the blue skies, and here on planet earth the Sepah seemingly left us alone.

Unbeknownst to Baba jan, that would be his last farewell to his beloved country. Like many prominent Jewish Iranian businessmen, he never returned.

Today, if the walls of the Palace and Tower could talk, they would weep tears of joy and sorrow. Happiness from the fond memories of poets and titans who paid homage to these great sites and even gifted souvenirs to be remembered.

Farewell to the 23,000 books left in pristine condition inside the Palace and without a friend to read. Despair for an ancient Jewish language that had been orally passed down for 2,700 years, only to vanish in a snap. Grief for the illustrious gowns once worn by Queen Farrah that hang on headless mannequins inside these historic landmarks to signify the death of a dynasty.

Dear friends, may you rest in peace.

The Escape Artist

Firoozeh and I built a beautiful mansion on Pahlavi Street. Giant Palm Trees paved our driveway, and Greek pillars formed a ring around our home. Inside, we walked on thick Italian marble, and every faucet was gold plated.

The Atrium Room was my favorite. It was two stories high and shaped in a circle. The roof *and* walls were glazed and adorned. Inside, I looked beyond the glass and admired my magnificent courtyard.

Our driver, cook, and maids each had their separate quarters.

I bought the land for 1,250,000 Toman and spent 3,000,000 Toman to build.

The property was completed on June 1, 1979.

We never slept in our new home. I was pressed to sell and flee.

Mr. Shirazi, an Iranian Jewish broker, hastily found us a buyer. He was the grandchild of the most cruel-hearted leader of the Islamic Regime. I named him the "Devil's Grandson."

On June 5, 1979, Firoozeh and I met Mr. Shirazi and the Devil's Grandson at the Escrow Office. My wife and I intended to close the sale and leave Iran the next day. Mr. Shirazi knew of our plan.

To my innocent surprise, the Devil's Grandson was short 100,000 Toman, and he asked for a discount. Young and desperate to flee, Firoozeh and I graciously obliged.

After our price reduction, our "buyer" and Mr. Shirazi stepped outside. Stinking of tobacco, Mr. Shirazi returned and said the "buyer" is short *anothe*r 100,000 Toman. I knew that the Devil's Grandson knew of our escape plan.

We feared the Devil's Grandson, his family, and the entire Islamic Regime. Although I held title to a mansion on Pahlavi Street, the tables were reversed.

Firoozeh and I reluctantly transferred 50% ownership to our "buyer." In return, he postdated a check for 60,000 Toman and rendered 100,000 Toman cash. I entrusted my best friend with that check.

The next day, I arrived at Tehran Airpot with my wife, two children, and one luggage stashed with cash.

The Sepah, comprised of young men that were eager to prove their worth to the Islamic Regime, controlled all entries and exits with an iron fist.

In line to board Swissair, I held Jasmine, and Firoozeh embraced Ezra. Gradually, we approached the queue's neck.

For *some* reason, the unassuming man in front of me walked away, and I had clear visibility of the dangerous affairs that awaited. My heart beat exponentially loud, and I was positive that everyone heard especially my innocent baby girl.

The Sepah guarded a list or more aptly put, the "blacklist." Once in front, families relinquished their passports, which were then carefully cross-checked to the names on the list.

In those long moments, the passports *and* families alike were the property of the Islamic Regime.

I recalled Firoozeh's maiden name on her passport. I conceived, it was inevitable that they find a match between her last name and her father's.

To fan the flames, many Jews identified on the blacklist were considered Zionist spies, and I recalled my Jewish last name. I conceived, it was inevitable that they'll fabricate a match and frame us for Israeli espionage.

In a flash, I told Firoozeh to remove her gold necklace. It was 24 Karats and also her anniversary gift. Of course, she refused. I grabbed Ezra and murmured, "Don't make trouble."

She steadily unhooked the clasp and hid the necklace inside her left fist. We stood shoulder to shoulder, and she snuck her necklace inside my right suit pocket.

We finally arrived at the front of the line. I grasped the necklace and passports inside my pocket. Firoozeh hugged Jasmine, and I held onto my son.

Time stood still when the guards saluted a handsome pilot that was decked in royal blue strutting our way. He looked debonair in the manner that he simultaneously smirked and nodded as if to deliberately render a mediocre salutation.

Our Swissair Captain ("the Captain") was followed by a band of beautiful and European stewardesses primped in makeup and high heels.

When he stylishly turned his head from side to side, his pilot's hat revealed gold wings, and when he stared straight on, everyone saw its sharp vinyl brim audaciously protruding forward.

His smart ensemble and gorgeous entourage exuded a proven authority that even the most sinister ridden guards respected.

My attention returned to our dire fate when suddenly the Captain flashed a big smile and jolted, "Doctor!" Besides myself, I faked a happy, familiar smile.

He removed his military aviators and introduced himself, "I'm Ali. Your patient." I vaguely remembered. To save *his* face, I replied, *"Chah-ke-reh-tam"* ("I am at your service" in Farsi).

He glanced at my return ticket and hurried us along *past* the guards.

On board, I unclenched my fist and released the necklace inside my pocket. A mere fond memory had saved my family.

Six hours later, we arrived in London. Two weeks later, we left London for Israel.

Just when I thought we had dodged our last bullet, one roared at full speed.

The Sepah charged into my best friend's home and demanded the Devil's Grandson's check. I am grateful that my best friend forfeited the money and saved his own life.

By the time the Iranian Hostage Crisis erupted, we were safe in America, and I never looked back.

"Thriller"

It was a sunny and quiet Thursday afternoon in 1985. I was seven years old and alone inside my grandparents' home. My mom telephoned and said that she was downstairs in the lobby. My grandparents live in a swanky high-rise along the Wilshire Corridor-a neighborhood in L.A. with the most exclusive residential towers.

Eager to press all of the buttons and descend 20 floors, I hastily tied my sneakers and packed my crayons. The house door was hefty and made of solid cherry wood. So with all of my grit and might, I yanked it wide open.

At that exact moment, HE opened his door. We stared at each other, and I screamed! Naturally, he shrieked back, and his voice carried. I was enthralled and bubbling with excitement.

It was Michael Jackson in the flesh. My heart beat rhythmically to "Beat it," my pelvis shook like "Dirty Diana," and in unison the rest of my inner workings moonwalked. A gigantic, black bodyguard stood strong, and yet he didn't scare me. To my sudden surprise, Michael swiftly made a slick 180, opened his door, and slammed it shut. I heard the nervous sound of the lock. He was never to be seen, or so I thought.

I mimicked the same and forgot about my mom. At this point, I heard train tracks traveling from one ear to the next. I felt anxious, and time stood still. Eleven minutes later, the doorbell rang, and I gasped.

It's the FBI! I'm surprised that I heard myself think. *I'm Iranian AND I terrorized Michael!* Undoubtedly, I was in double the trouble. With coverage of the Iranian Hostage Crisis still fresh in the American consciousness and collective memory, this was not the "Thriller" that I had imagined!

If I may, Michael (I loved calling him by his first name), was neighbors with my grandparents. Their cherry wood door and his stood 10 feet apart, and their living room and his shared a common wall. For many years, I heard Micheal rehearse his magnificent hits. My ears witnessed his notorious "ow"'s and "ah"'s, and my soles felt the remnant tremors of his dance steps. It all felt like a jubilant earthquake.

I had begged to meet him. But just like the apple in the story of Creation, he was the forbidden and very famous fruit.

The doorbell continued to ring, and it had a royal tone. It began with a high pitched chime and ended low. I put my index fingers inside my ears. *I'm too young to get arrested!* I feared that my grandparents would get evicted, and the ripple effect that it would cast on all of the other Iranian grandparents at the Wilshire Corridor.

I felt the weight of the world on my tiny shoulders, and the ringing exasperated my energy until there was an eerie pause followed by a gentle knock. I closed my eyes and reluctantly faced my destiny. This time, I heard a soft voice say, "Hi." I opened my eyes, and he stood bashfully behind his bodyguard. The FBI was nowhere to be seen. Michael handed his guard a sealed yellow envelope who then passed it to me, and after that they left.

I watched him leave. The iridescent lights formed a psychedelic rainbow, shaped like a halo, that magically followed Michael to the elevator. Once again, I shut the door and hastily tore open the flap.

There it was. In all its pomp and circumstance. A black and white, 12 x 12 signed autograph. "Love always, Michael."

Purim

That morning in 1986 I felt extraordinary. It was Purim, and I was Queen Esther. ("Purim" is a Jewish holiday that was set in Ancient Persia. The heroine, Esther, saved the Jewish people from death by the King's evil viceroy. Coined the "Jewish Halloween," it is customary for kids to dress up as characters of the Purim story. Once a poor Jewish girl, Esther ultimately rose to become the Queen of Persia.)

I crimped by bangs and donned a floral wreath. My frosty pink satin gown glowed in the dark, and thick tulle hid underneath. My dress featured a ruffled, off-the-shoulder lacy neckline.

The car honked, and that was my cue. I strutted out the front door, and my Mom feverishly followed. She threw red rose petals over me and cheered, *"Aroos beshi eenshallah!"* ("One day become a bride God willing!" in Farsi).

Strutting down my royal red carpet, I sashayed along the periphery of our garden. There, she turned on the hose and poured water behind me for good luck.

In doing so, my Mom ululated a high-pitched *"lililili!"* and woke up the entire neighborhood. ("Ululation" is a loud, wavering vocal sound with rapid back and forth tongue movement performed by Middle-Eastern women in celebrations, and of course in movies when one wants to highlight the primitive nature of Middle Eastern culture.)

I completed my final loop, and within the same range of motion I moseyed down our stone-paved driveway. Her lililili's triumphantly followed. Meanwhile, watchdogs howled while my neighbor, Mrs. Peterson, stared in horror. I reckoned that she was disappointed because we "wasted" water in the highly publicized drought of the '80s.

The lililili's became louder and faster. Yet, I maintained a snail's pace until I reached the bottom where He waited.

He lifted my train, and I stepped inside the passenger's seat. I skillfully applied cherry-flavored lip-gloss for my finishing touch. I looked to him and boldly said, "Step on the gas."

He blasted Neil Diamond's "I'm Coming to America" with his suave Iranian flair. The cool wind blew in my hair, and my smile shined from ear-to-ear. Our eyes gazed at one another, and I gleamed in euphoria. Together forever, we sang out loud.

My Dad driving carpool was my favorite time of the day.

We made a fast turn onto Rockingham Avenue, and he reached to mute the stereo's volume. I placed my hand over his and said, "Not today Dad. It's Purim." He smiled back, and time stood still.

I knew that we had reached our destination when I saw the cold-looking gated mansion. There, stood Stacey and her mother, Suzy.

They embodied perfection. They had sun-kissed hair, button-noses, and golden skin.

Stacey's tight, high ponytail stayed bouncy all day. She styled her school uniforms and launched a la mode trends like 80's mainstays of sky-high hairspray and the popped polo shirt collar.

Suzy wore leotards and pastel colors. Together, they exuded a menacing, elitist flair.

Like an army of bees circling a hive, Suzy suspiciously swarmed around my Dad's car. *What did she expect to find? A bomb seemingly disguised as chelo-kabab?* ("Chelo-Kabab" are Persian meat skewers served with rice.)

She was perturbed by us. Like her, we were Jews, yet a different breed. In her eyes, we were poor, dark-skinned, loud, illiterate, primitive, and hairy.

Our "otherness" was illuminated to me by the questions that she would ask in carpool. Such as, "Do you plan to return to Iran?"

She peeked through the driver's window, and my Dad waved hello. He offered her pistachios and raisins. She scoffed at his Persian variant of trail mix.

I had ants in my pants (figuratively) and anticipated my grand entrance at school. Finally, Stacey entered our car, and I waved goodbye to Suzy.

I turned my head about and smiled, "Happy Purim."

She did a double sniff in a snobbish way and said, "Your car smells." I grinned confidently, "That's my Mom's *ghormeh sabzi*." ("Gormeh Sabzi" is a Persian stew with a distinct fenugreek aroma.)

Then, she twirled her index finger clockwise and asked, "What are you?" I adjusted my wreath and lifted my chin. "Queen Esther," I replied proudly. She looked appalled. I reckoned that Stacey was embarrassed because she forgot to wear her costume.

The pot of ghormeh sabzi shook and rattled the entire way.

My Dad steadily drove up a flowery hill, filled with daisies that looked picturesque, and carefully minded the speed bumps. The steel gate that was grandiose in size opened slowly. The scent of daisies ran wild through the air. My fancy Jewish day school was built like an iron fortress atop a mountain that oversaw the palatial estates of Beverly Hills.

I kissed my Dad and seized my belongings. I ran past Stacey to the Girl's Locker Room. Hastily, I reached inside my Ralph's paper bag for the "holy grail"- my crinoline.

At lightning speed, I unzipped my gown and slipped it on. The crinoline fit snug around my waist. Without breaking a sweat, I zipped up my dress and raced out.

Like a deserted boat drifting aimlessly in the sea, my ginormous, poofy gown rocked back and forth as I glided toward Mrs. Berger's third-grade class.

I walked through the classroom door sideways. If "dead silence" had a face, it was the vapid look on each student and Mrs. Berger. *Did I miss the memo?* Because everyone dressed in school uniform. Once again, I was the outsider.

Red as a tomato, my mind traveled back in time to Free-Dress Day.

I wore candy-apple-red leather pants made famous by Michael in "Thriller." Bright and early, I sat on our plastic-covered, silky beige sofa. The sun shined on my face through our French windows.

At the top of the hour, my Dad clapped his hands and said, *"Yalla!"* ("Let's go!" in Arabic). I jumped for joy, well not *really*.

Many hours later, my leather pants stuck like glue to the sofa's plastic cover. With two hands, I gripped my Dad's arm, and he pulled me up like slowly peeling a strip of wax off hairy skin.

In the car, we laughed at my heart-shaped, sweaty butt-print that was embossed on the sofa's seat.

At drop-off, Rabbi Gooz spotted my outfit and followed me to class. (For the record, "gooz" means "fart" in Farsi. Rabbi Gooz or shall I say, Rabbi Fart, is her fake name but befitting nonetheless.)

Rabbi Gooz had called the seventh-grade girls "prick-tease" because their pleated skirts were too short.

She was 6 feet tall and had feet the size of a men's 11 shoe. Her round, blonde hair looked like a chia pet. Legend has it that Rabbi Gooz tackled Benny Benjamin for the last jelly donut on the day of his Bar Mitzvah, and he never made it to his *Haftarah* (the section from the Prophets that is read by a Bar/Bat Mitzvah child).

In class, she pointed at me, and everyone stared in silence. Fear-stricken, I slowly got up. The chair's legs screeched, and my leather pants made a loud crinkly noise.

She yelled, "Your pants violate the dress-code!" I crossed my legs and peed in my pants. Shamefaced, my skin turned as purple as a dried eggplant that Persians use in a variety of stews. Thankfully, my leather pants were skin-tight, and not even one drop of pee hit the floor.

Rabbi Gooz escorted me outside, and the children's laughter ensued inside. She forbade me to return to class. I sat on the hot concrete and waited for my Mom.

Mrs. Berger said, "You're tardy." I returned to the physical world after daydreaming my real-life nightmare. It was too late to run, and thus I stayed.

I shuffled sideways between rows of tables that were configured horizontally into impossibly challenging pathways. I was trapped inside a wicked maze, and everyone enjoyed staring. The dead silence deviously lingered until I reached an empty seat in the back, and Mrs. Berger picked up where she had left.

I sat down, and my gown involuntarily lifted. In a blink, I pressed it down and prayed. *Dear God, please watch over me today.* My hands stayed put and kept the feisty crinoline at bay.

At P.E. ("Physical Education"), I followed Coach's orders and ran the track. I nearly completed one lap, when I tripped over my crinoline and sprained my right ankle.

Humiliated, I held in my tears. Coach rushed over with ice and water. Once again, I sat on the hot concrete and waited for my Mom.

Her car pulled up, and I limped over. I saw my reflection in the passenger window. I merely impersonated Frida Kahlo on her Quinceañera.

I told her the truth, "Rabbi Gooz and I were the only ones in costume." She held my hand and kissed me.

Did Queen Esther have it this rough? I fathomed that she did. Like me, Esther was Jewish and Persian. She escaped death, and I escaped Khomeini. I was a modern-day Queen Esther, skillfully attempting to navigate the evil decrees of Jewish Day School, when all that I really wanted was to be accepted unconditionally.

Khastegari

I was 14 years old, and Junior Prom was two weeks away. That morning in History class, a mysterious envelope and a red rose sat on my desk.

Everybody stared in shock. I tried to stay calm, yet my legs trembled. I tore open the sealed flap, and in the blink of an eye, I read the note.

THE David Colby asked me to be his date! The thought of kissing him made me weak in the knees. In study hall, I passed him a secret note. It screamed, "Yes!"

That night, I shared my newly found success with my Dad, and he said, "Out of the question." Heavily distraught, I urgently asked, "Why?" He replied, "What will people think?"

I begged him and said, "I like David." He replied, "You are too young to have a boyfriend." I plead for my life and cried, "We are not in Iran!" He rhetorically asked, "And, the American way is better?"

I saw the tension in his warm eyes, and I recalled my fifth Birthday at Roxbury Park.

My Dad decorated the trees with pink balloons and white ribbons. It was magnificent.

Suddenly, a Park Ranger appeared from the bushes and asked, "Where is your permit?" *Who knew we needed one?*

The heartless Ranger carefully watched my Dad dismantle everything, and I cried as it unfolded.

The August heat made him more tired, and I remembered my Dad's loving eyes.

Before my friends arrived, he prepared a beautiful picnic on the green grass. Once again, he saved the day.

Like my fifth Birthday, my Dad crafted a plan to make everyone happy. He said, "First, I have to meet David's parents."

In Persian culture, if a man wanted to date a woman for marriage, his family would visit her family. The man brought flowers, and the woman offered hot tea, sweets, and fruit. This phenomenon is called *"Khastegari."*

I went on my first Khastegari at age 14.

I carried a huge bouquet, and David's parents graciously greeted us.

Inside, we sat in-between our parents, opposite one another. David gently waived and whispered, "Hi." My heart melted.

His mom offered me chocolate chip cookies, and my mouth watered for a tasty bite. I nearly reached for a sweet when my Mom pinched me to *taarof,* and I politely said, "No." (In Persian etiquette, "Taarof" requires a guest to initially decline food and drinks so as not to appear greedy.)

Our novice parents were nervous and made small talk. They glanced at us for inspiration.

I uttered the first thought that came to my mind. "I like your sneakers." David replied, "I like your dress." I upped my game and said, "I like you."

We courageously broke the ice. My parents finished their iced-teas, and we left shortly.

With my Dad's blessing, I went to Junior Prom with David and had the time of my life.

Twenty years later, I saw him at a charity ball in Los Angeles. We said hello and goodbye. After, he turned around and said, "You had the coolest dad." I replied, "I do."

Risky Business Inside the Vatican

I was 19 years old, and I decided to study abroad in Italy. Early Sunday morning, I arrived at Vatican City. Out of nowhere, a sweet, little nun gave me a ticket. It read: *"Vaticano, V.I.P."* ("Vatican, V.I.P." in Italian). She hand gestured to follow her, and I did.

There was a long line to enter. Mostly men, they were impeccably dressed and smelled delicious. Inside, the sweet nun disappeared amid the cloud of intoxicating cologne.

A peculiar man followed me at a short distance. Naively, I didn't mind. I knew that I stood out. I was American, a woman, and dressed in Levi's.

I named him, *"L'uomo Strano"* or "Strange Man." He wore a navy quilted jacket, black slim-fit trousers, and leather brown penny loafers. He had silver hair and black eyes.

He uttered, *"Principessa*, you're American." ("Principessa" is "Princess" in Italian.) I sheepishly nodded, "Yes."

In a blink's eye, there were 1000 flashes. I followed the clicking sounds and flickering lights, and I couldn't believe my naked eyes.

I aggressively pushed thru the crowd and yelled, *"Scusi!" "Scusi!"* ("Excuse me!" "Excuse me!" in Italian).

I stood in awe. I got so close that I nearly pinched his chubby cheeks. It was Pope John Paul II.

Suddenly, I sensed a strange "touch." I removed my Casio camera from my face and turned my head. There was no one. Two short moments later, it happened again, and the brush was against my buttocks.

This time, I completely turned around. Face-to-face with L'uomo Strano, he flashed me a dirty smirk. He hid his hands inside his pockets and gently thrusted his groin. I looked down and saw his bulge. I froze there like a deer in headlights while my face turned bloody red, and my ears burned. I only heard my beating heart.

I wanted to scream *"PERICOLO!"* ("DANGER!" in Italian). But, I feared that it would put me in more jeopardy.

Still in shock, I looked up. This time, L'uomo Strano smiled, and I saw his yellow, rotten teeth. He whispered raunchy Italian gibberish. Thankfully, I got shoved by a photographer and ran to the exit.

Outside, I saw my roommate Celeste. I screamed, "I'm so happy to see you!" She swerved her hips side to side and admired her fake wedding band. Celeste was a devout Catholic.

I shared my scary story, and she blamed me. "It's because you wear tight Levi's." She removed her ring and held it to my face when she bursted out loud, "That's why I wear this!"

We walked back to the bus, and I remained silent. *Was the touch and go really my fault?*

Celeste didn't keep quiet. In a jealous rage, she repeated, "How come YOU saw the Pope!?" After all, she was the Catholic and I was the Jew, whose salvation was uncertain, let alone by His Holiness the Pope.

The bus was filled with Italians of every generation who were all now suspect. I deliberately tied my pink sweater around my waist and stood guard like a merciless watchdog.

Lo and behold, Celeste shared my holy debacle with a mob of rambunctious teenagers. It spread like wildfire, and every passenger became green with envy.

Italians can go a lifetime without ever seeing the Pope in person. Yet, here I was, a Persian Jewish girl from Los Angeles, sweeping up their lifelong dream like the person who's in line ahead of you at a gas station winning the Mega Lottery.

The Crooked Rabbi

In 2014, I was 36 years old and unmarried. Esther, my mom's Kaballah teacher, begged me to visit Rabbi Shmuel. She had a raspy voice and spewed, *"Cheshet zadan!"* ("You are cursed!" in Farsi). She trusted Rabbi Shmuel's mystic powers and repeated, "Only HE can remove the evil spell!" Come hell or high water, I emphatically declined until my voicemail went haywire, and I surrendered like a chump.

Rabbi Shmuel was porky and smoked a Camel Light. His white blouse was skin-tight and partly untucked. The middle button was undone, and I reluctantly caught site of his hairy belly. His black suit was covered in patches of white dust, and of course one sneaker was untied. I still gave him the benefit of the doubt and entered the lion's den.

He blew smoke and uttered his first words. "Why are you single?" I took the witness stand and replied, "Where is my besheret?"

He looked down at his right foot and spotted the neglected shoelace. He shrugged it off and asked, "How are you living? It's the saddest thing. This sleeping alone." Before I testified, he interrupted. "With whom do you eat breakfast?" I remained calm and answered, "Myself." His judgment palpable, "That is very sad."

The storefront was bare and sealed. Inside, the place felt unholy. The kitchen was tiny, and the restroom had a leaky faucet and green gooey soap. There were rows and rows of empty tables.

He sniffled as he stroked his grey beard. Still baffled, he commented, "I can't understand." He stared at me and said, "Tell me your birth date and last three addresses." I indulged him. Suddenly, he opened a large Jewish book, and his fat fingers feverishly swept its pages. He looked up ghastly and said, "You will have children." I asked, "What about marriage?" His voice became monotone, and he muttered, "I don't see that."

I succumbed to this lunatic and cried. "But why me?" He apologized. "Love is a gift, and it's not for all." I heard *and* listened. "What have I done?" His answers became worse. "You are special." I was hypnotized. "Help me, Rabbi!" He paused and said, "Give me two-hundred dollars, and I will have more answers." I gladly obliged.

He gestured me toward the exit and unlocked the door. He said, "Every morning, set a beautiful table for yourself with fruit, juice, coffee, and eggs." Eyes wide shut and ears wide open, I asked, "What then?" He replied, "Then, you need to smoke a cigarette."

I strangled him with my naked hands and beat him with the heavy Jewish book. Then, I pierced an earlobe with his lit cigarette. I nearly killed him until I snapped out of my murder fantasy.

I murmured like a smooth criminal, "I want to be healthy and smoke-free so that I *can* marry and have children."

With that, I turned my heels and left without saying goodbye. I happily never returned.

Change Your Place, Change Your Luck

"Summer Loving Happened so Fast"

What began as a summer holiday in Tel Aviv, became a tapestry of beautiful events that were interwoven by the hidden hand of *Hashem* ("Hashem" is "God" in Hebrew) to bring me to this moment today.

It was September 14, 2015, the second night of *Rosh Hashanah* (Jewish New Year), and I was on holiday in my favorite city in the world, Tel Aviv. I rented a colorful and cheerful apartment on Spinoza Street. The balcony had a yellow vinyl chair, a tiny cotton hammock, and cigarette butts everywhere doused in red lipstick.

The terrace was embedded in a million Jasmine flowers. I couldn't help but ponder the serendipity between the flower's name and mine.

That afternoon, I sunbathed at Gordon Beach and received a text: "I'm here." It was my friend Eva from Los Angeles.

I ran barefoot on the sizzling sand and then onto the scorching concrete of Dizengoff Street. I barely kept my coverup. I greeted Eva with open arms and blisters.

I was blown away. The other night, Eva had said that she may visit. I never dreamed that it would be possible.

She joined Dina, our local barista, for coffee and cigarettes. They joked and laughed hysterically. Yet, neither one understood the other. I had arrived just in time.

Eva wore stonewashed daisy dukes, and I loved the way that her rhinestone army boots sparkled day and night. She matched them with a vintage Aerosmith jersey, and underneath it all she had a crochet bikini. She was sun-kissed and beautiful.

Dina rocked a sleeve tattoo of roses and Madonna. She had jet black hair with pink highlights. She served a rich Turkish coffee and slipped me a Parliament Slim Thin. I felt like a celebrity.

That night, through my cousin Assaf, we were invited to a holiday party that was hosted by his friend Leor.

Upon arriving at the party, Eva spotted a handsome gentleman standing on a platform, whom she thought was Leor. He had a high and tight buzz cut, and he wore a white crew-neck. She grabbed my hand, and we charged forward. She yelled, "Leor! We're the American girls!"

We hastily crossed the empty dance floor and ran up a flight of stairs. Everyone stared. I wore five-inch wedges and held onto the railings for dear life.

He shook his head and said, "I don't know you." Eva was dumbfounded and said, "Turn around and pretend this never happened." I seized the tail end of my maxi dress and raced down faster than I came up. We sat incognito at the bar and drank champagne. Several minutes later, he came and introduced himself. "I'm Amir."

It turned out, this handsome gentleman was not Leor, but in fact, it was my future husband (Amir), and Leor was his best friend.

Across the bar, Eva captured Ronen's eyes. He was a goofy divorcee and loved to giggle. Ronen was tall, dark, and good-looking.

That night, the moon and stars were arranged in divine order to bring the four of us together. We even met a politician ("the Politician"). He wore thick spectacles and had yellow veneers. His voice bellowed, and he laughed at his own jokes. The Politician urged Amir to conjure up war stories to melt my heart, and Amir ignored him.

At a quarter past 2 a.m., all of us including the Politician packed inside a *shirut* (shared taxi minivan) and headed to Rothschild Boulevard. The shirut played 90's techno and was lit with fluorescent disco lights. On our way, we picked up a lone soldier and an eccentric bag lady. Without a thought or word, Amir offered his seat, and she accepted. Everyone idly stared at each other and said nothing.

We approached the Penguin, an underground club, and Amir knew the bouncer. He was mean-looking and held a pistol. We cut the line and entered a tunnel. Pitch dark and airless, Amir held my hand, and the music led us.

Dark and smoky inside, the club was uninhibited. People danced very close together and shared kisses.

Eli spotted Eva and me first. By then, the Politician had disappeared; Ronen returned to his *moshav* ("Israeli farm village" in Hebrew); and Amir kissed me goodnight.

The D.J. played Dolly Parton's "Jolene." This time, I grabbed Eva's hand, and we danced with all of our heart and soul. Eli was fascinated by us.

He was husky and had diamond blue eyes. He spoke perfect English, which he attributed to the lyrics of Ice-T. He loved his Raiders hat, and on his forearm he had a ginormous tattoo of the Star of David.

After "Jolene" ended, we cajoled the D.J. to play the song like a broken record. Until no one remained, but for the defeated disc jockey and Eva, Eli, and me.

Eli walked us to the exit and returned inside. We knew that we will see him again.

The sun was especially bright, and it caught our eyes. We tried to catch a cab but our efforts were futile. One-by-one, they rejected us. We walked miles barefoot and sweat like pigs. Passersby stared suspiciously, and mothers hovered over their children. I was baffled. Until suddenly, a driver shouted, *"Sharmutot!"* ("Sluts!" in Hebrew).

Eva screamed back, "Racists!" I laughed so hard that I felt chest pain. "Eva! They think we are prostitutes!"

I grabbed hold of the mirror hanging adrift at the *limonanas* (lemonade infused with mint) stand. "See for yourself!" I shoved it in her face then mine.

Our mascara was bleeding. My hair looked like Medusa's with the writhing serpents, and our pupils were bloodshot like the Devil's eyes. I resembled a lady of the night that had just committed a crime of passion.

Eva shouted, "It's because we are Americans! I will sue Israel!" She nervously looked inside her purse and screamed, "I deserve a ride! I flew a thousand miles!" She lit a cigarette and waited for a miracle.

I walked back home. For the first time, I was unshaken by people's judgments. I was a foreigner who was standing shoeless in broad daylight at a congested Israeli intersection and unleashed from the omnipresent, downward gaze of Persian Jewish society. "Hallelujah!" I was free at last.

Opportunity Knocks

During that same summer holiday in Israel, before Amir and I ever even met, I met my father's friend, Elan, and his wife for lunch. Unbeknownst to me, Elan was a partner at a prominent U.S. firm and specialized in U.S. tax law. At that lunch, he explained to me his profession and asked about mine in the United States. I replied, "The same as yours." I guess he liked my answer, and on the spot he asked if I would like to work for his company in Israel.

By all accounts, I did not apply for a job, nor did I even consider relocation.

To the contrary-this was supposed to be a short stint in Israel on the trajectory of returning to Los Angeles and resuming my normal life in the Persian Jewish bubble.

In fact, upon his offer, I almost fell off of my chair and quite frankly laughed. I then asked myself, *Here I am on vacation, how and why in the world did this opportunity so effortlessly land at my doorstep?* I did not have an answer but in hindsight it was all part of God's divine plan for me.

I returned to Los Angeles and seriously weighed the pros and cons of such a drastic, life-altering relocation. My Iranian parents, unequivocally wished that I would stay put. They asked, "We escaped the Middle East and you want to return?" Still without an answer to my question, in January 2016 I decided to accept the offer and embark on a new, adventurous chapter in the land of Israel, which proved to be the best decision that I have ever made.

One may label my meeting Amir as simply a case of misidentification, plain coincidence, or sheer luck. I beg to differ. Our meeting coupled with my offer at the firm was destiny. It required a master plan from Hashem, divine in inspiration and design, that neither Amir nor I could ever concoct ourselves. It is only when I stood underneath my magnificent *chuppah* (canopy under which Jewish marriages are performed), did I have the answer to my question. It was because I was meant to be in Israel to begin our courtship. In Hebrew, they say, *"meshaneh makom, meshaneh mazal."* Change your place, change your luck, and I sure did.

I will always remember the first time that I saw Amir. He stood by himself with his hands in both pockets and slowly moving side to side to the beat of the background music. He looked so cool.

Within minutes of meeting him, my heart and soul told me that I must get and keep his attention, no matter what.

In a sea of stunning Israeli women, he stayed by my side that night, and now I will stay by his side forever.

I'm a Jew, I Swear!

The waiting room felt claustrophobic, and it was packed with nefarious looking immigrants. With only two seats, I sat on the floor and met eyes with a mafia gangster from Russia. I named him "Nikolay the Avenger." He was twenty-something and bald. He squatted from time-to-time and wore a velour Adidas tracksuit.

Mr. Nikolay the Avenger ate barbecue sunflowers seeds like an Olympic sport. In rhythmic motions, he popped them into his mouth and sucked its flavors. His tongue glided across and pushed the seeds between his molars. Then, his teeth firmly pressed down and voila! The seeds cracked open like a hatched egg. He targeted the trash bin and spit the shells. Each time, he aimed perfectly.

*Why did he come to Israel? S*urely, he did not "look Jewish." In fact, no one did at the airport's quarantine.

After a long time, a security agent screamed, *"Yasmeen!"* ("Jasmine!"), and I jumped for joy! Finally, I was free, or so I thought.

He led me into an even tinier room with a ceiling fan that looked dangerously frightful. It was set on "high," and its blades shook and wobbled violently. I feared that one may strike me.

I only heard the fan's noisy humming when suddenly a female officer shouted, "Take a seat!" Her wish was my command, and the other agent departed inconspicuously.

I begged the question, "Why am I here?" She answered in a monotone utterance, "Just protocol."

She scrupulously opened my passport and began her line of questioning.

"Did you have a bat-mitzvah?"
"Yes."

"So you are Jewish?"
"Yes."

"But you were born in Iran?"
"Yes."

"Are your parents Jewish?"
"Yes."

"Do you travel to Iran?"
"No."

"Do you have an Iranian passport?"
"No."

"Have you changed your name?"
"No."

"Tenk you. Vait here." ("Thank you. Wait here.")

She pushed her seat, and it made a shrilling screech. When she opened the door there stood a male agent. They huddled, and spoke about me in Hebrew. Then, she patted his shoulder and scurried along.

I tried to make eye contact, but his eyeglasses were foggy. Inevitably, I stared at his overgrown chin while he asked me questions.

"Do you know anyone in Iran?"
"No."

"Do you speak Arabic?"
"No."

"Do you have a Hebrew name?"
"Yes. Sigalit."

Like his forerunner, Agent Four-Eyes never smiled. I felt like a guilty criminal, but unsure what crime I had committed. After, he stood up and said, "Tenk you. Vait here."

He opened the door and lo and behold, stood the fourth agent. They whispered, and he gave her a pat on the back.

She was a meaty redhead and wore high heels. When she walked, the floors rumbled, and her heels made a vexing clonking sound. The "click-clack" of her heels joined forces with the "humming" of the fan, and I was rattled more than ever.

Like her predecessors, she asked questions, and I answered without thinking.

We played a game of tag-team. Except, I was the only rookie player on my team who was up against a tailgate of Israeli clandestine professionals.

Agent Redhead closed her notebook and declared, "You are free." Just one hitch, I had spent hours in captivity, and I forgot my final destination. I was remiss to ask my interrogators for a helping hand.

I left the underground basement and wandered aimlessly. The airport was a ghost town. My luggage sat idly in the center of the El Al carousel. Finally, I collected myself *and* my belongings, and I caught a late-night cab to Tel Aviv.

In the cab, I took a trip down memory lane when I rode Colossus at Magic Mountain.

First, the roller coaster gradually ascended. As it reached the sky, it abruptly jolted and stopped in its tracks. I looked down from high above, and everything resembled tiny ants. Nothing happened, just yet. One second remained until my daring first plunge. I was filled with fear, adventure, and excitement.

I had an inkling that my experience at Ben Gurion Airport was the beginning of a wild roller coaster ride in *Eretz Israel* ("The Land of Israel" in Hebrew).

Slumlord Millionaire

I left my hotel with great expectations when Shimon, the real estate broker, confirmed our meeting: "19:00. 72 Arlozorov."

I arrived, and hundreds had huddled outside. I feared the absolute worst-a deadly bomb! I had a choice to stay and save my new apartment, or leave and save my life. It was a tricky decision.

I dialed Shimon, and the calls dropped.

I pushed and shoved my way up to the front line. There, a petite twenty-something kept the crowd at bay. I named her the "General."

I politely said, "Excuse me, I have an appointment." The General chuckled arrogantly as she pointed at the masses. "Everyone here has an appointment."

That conniving demon broker! There was no real bomb threat. He had procured a blind-date with me and all of Tel Aviv!

I pushed and shoved my way back. The building stood like a tiny speck in the far distance. I sat in the freezing cold air for one agonizing hour. Yet, the line made headways slower than a tortoise on *Giligan's Island* (American sitcom).

The General shouted into the megaphone, *"Rah-bo-tay!"* ("People!" in Hebrew) "We have a winner!"

The mob booed and cheered. They chanted, "Shimi!" "Shimi!" "Shimi!"

Shimon appeared on the horizon and stood up on stacked milk crates. He shouted, "Follow me *chevre*!" ("Chevre" is "my friends" in Hebrew.) "Your castles await!" Like sheep, they followed.

It was like the scene from *Gladiator*, where Maximus killed his enemies and shouted, "Are you not entertained!" Despite his brutality, the crowd idolized him.

I remained and reflected. *That's it? But, where will I live?*

I bid farewell and departed. I passed the Carmel Market and saw a graffiti mural of two cacti desperados, pointing their pistols at a cowboy. The cowboy looked Mexican also the sombrero and mustache. Yet, a "Tel Aviv" sign stood between his legs.

The artist paid tribute to the Wild West in the Land of Milk and Honey (Israel), *and* Tel Aviv was truly the Wild, Wild West!

Still in last night's clothes, I roamed the streets like a Las Vegas hooker on the prowl for my next prey.

My blood sugar was at an all-time low, and I had an inflamed canker sore. I made a pit stop outside Ben Yehuda 20, and as luck may find me, I spotted a listing. It read: "Call Tzvika for Rent."

Tzvika, the landlord, arrived at a drop of a dime! He had silver hair and was plump. He wore a baby blue, short-sleeve button-down and khakis.

The apartment was the size of a shoebox, and the kitchen was a sink. The steel bars secured the bedroom window, and one neighbor was a middle-aged, single woman. I named her "Cat Lady."

Yet, Tzvika was charming. He said, "You are precious like a diamond." My heart fluttered with his charming platitudes. He crossed his heart and swore, "This apartment is safe and working."

I "negotiated" at full-price and signed my life away!

That night, I took a shower in my new Tel Aviv apartment. The hot water gushed down my wounded body, and I was in pure ecstasy.

I fantasized about exotic caviar and succulent grapes when I suddenly heard three blasts. BOOM! BOOOM! BOOM! This time, I truly believed that it was a bomb.

I leaped out and landed in deep water, literally! The water heater had exploded!

I wrapped myself in a skimpy pool towel that I had borrowed from the hotel, and with shampoo frothing in my frizzy hair, I whizzed out!

I banged on doors, and no one answered. I saw water seeping through my front door. Desperate for help, I ran into the street.

A computer repair shop adjoined my building. I opened its door and screamed, "SOS!" (I figured, "SOS" is the international code for "Emergency.") The owner took one look and jolted past me! I hung onto my towel and chased after him.

He *knew* to run to my apartment. *Who was this mystery man?* Knee-deep in water, he dragged his legs to my bathroom. He turned off a switch, and it stopped raining.

The mystery man offered a handshake and said, "I'm Amos. Your neighbor." My left hand clung onto my towel, and my right greeted him.

Before he left, Amos said, "I will call Tzvika."

All the while, Cat Lady had snuck in. She was mute and dark-skinned, and her body moved like the Hunchback of Notre Dame.

Half-crouched and barefoot inside my bathroom, she scooped water with her dirty shoe. Bit by bit, she poured the water inside my over-flooded toilet.

Tzvika took his sweet time, and Amos returned with a bucket and spare clothes.

I scooped a bucket of water and passed it to Cat Lady. Hunched over in proper feline form, she carried it to Amos. Then, he dumped the bucket over my terrace and tossed the empty bucket back to Cat Lady. She caught it by its handle and slung it back to me. Once again, I scooped, she transferred, and he poured. We soldiered on this way until the water receded.

I dried the damp floors with my wimpy hotel towel when Tzvika arrived just in time.

I promised myself, *It's time this scoundrel got a taste of his own medicine*. Before Amos and Cat Lady's very eyes, I shouted, "I will report you to the Housing Authority!"

Tzvika "shushed" me in a delicate gesture and offered his soft hands. I suspiciously accepted, and he helped me up. Without hesitation, he gave my towel to Cat Lady, and she dried the floors.

Before I can shout another insult, he gently spoke. "You are too pretty to get mad." Taken aback by his well-rehearsed flattery, I recovered swiftly and yelled, "Tzvika, I'm wet!" He retorted frankly, "It's just water." Thus, he had an innocent answer for every allegation. Such as, "How can I know you take long showers?" I earnestly plead, "But Tzvika, I have curly hair."

He rebutted, "My showers are seven minutes." He pretended to shampoo and brush his teeth together and said, "You see, like this." I was beating a dead horse until he shared his "bright" idea. "Shower at Gordon Gym! I go there to take long showers!"

At that moment, I finally understood the bad card that I was dealt, and I capitulated.

Tzvika was the type of person who asked permission to kill, and his victims acquiesced to their own murders because Tzvika was showing them the road to hell on a gold paved carpet.

I imagined, in a mild and tender way, he revealed his deadly plot. "Yasmeen, you are so beautiful, and I hate to do this. But, may I kill you?" I replied, "Of course Tzvika and may I help?" I was a co-conspirator to my own homicide.

Tzvika left and took my towel with him.

Amos collected his bucket and turned to me. "Israel is not America. There's no *real* housing authority." Indeed he was right and not just about the housing authority.

Hot Tub Time Machine

I took Tzvika's unsolicited advice and joined Gordon Gym.

On my first day, I headed straight to the Ladies Locker Room. As advised, I took a long and steaming hot shower. Like kneading dough, I massaged conditioner into my scalp. All the while, the sizzling water cascaded over me, and my skin wrinkled like a dried up prune.

After my hydromassage, I put on my shower cap and robe.

Inside the locker room was a swinging door, which led to the Ladies spa.

An erotic mist arose from the hot tub and gradually swirled upwards, only to spin higher and vanish into thick air. Voluptuous jet bubbles erupted from all angles, and they shouted my name, "Yasmeen! Come hither!"

Better yet, I had the spa all to myself. In 80's style slow-motion, I removed my robe. Inch by inch, I carefully stepped into the jacuzzi, and my naked body jerked from the heat. At last, I was submerged.

Despite my best efforts, the steam room also enticed me.

I decided to quickly refresh myself inside the spa's walk-in shower. The freezing cold water stabbed me like falling ice pricks. Dripping wet and shivering, I tippy-toed to the steam.

The steam room was thick and dense like London fog. I pushed out my hands to navigate and moved at a snail's pace. I reached a seat and snuggled my legs into my chest. At last, I defrosted and decompressed, as I exhaled a huge sigh of relief and said out loud, *"Baruch Hashem"* ("Thank God" in Hebrew).

My eyelids were half-closed, when I heard, "Yasmeen?"

I jumped up! "Who's here!"

He answered, "It's Tamir."

Sweet Jesus, it's last week's blind date from Hell.

I screamed, "Why are you here!" In that instant, I forgot that I was stark naked.

An unfamiliar manly voice replied, "Same as you, and I'm Yossi."

Tamir insisted, *"Kapara*, why didn't you call me?" ("Kapara" is "sweetheart" in Hebrew.)

Yossi shouted, "SHE is the famous Yasmeen!"

Everything happened so fast. Alas, I knew that it was time to leave when Tamir said, "Kapara, this is the most naked I see you even in my dreams."

The cloudy haze gradually settled. Yossi and Tamir's silhouettes emerged, and so did mine! I slung open the door and dashed. I never returned to the *unisex* spa at Gordon Gym.

"I just knew"

I took a stroll down memory lane to the Penguin Club and met Eli. I gave him $3,000 in U.S. cash. He promised me a 1:4 exchange rate, "4" being the *Shekel* (Israeli Currency). It was a real bang for the buck.

Tomorrow came and went. So did the next three days and Eli had disappeared with my money.

It was *Erev Shabbat* ("Sabbath Eve" in Hebrew), and I took the last bus to Amir. Although he did not expect me, I had to see a familiar face.

The demographics inside Bus 4 was like the Human Rights Council at the United Nations.

I saw disillusioned Ethiopian Jews, frail Eritrean women, muscular Sudanese men, Israeli Arabs, flocks of ultra-orthodox Jews in the back, and herds of fancy Russian women in the front.

The ride was a wild goose chase, and I almost didn't make it. The bus moved at turbo speed, and I grasped my pole for dear life. Despite my best efforts, my body flung across the bus with every wild turn. After each fall, I immediately patted myself down and pushed and shoved my way back.

I arrived at Rothschild Boulevard scathed and bruised. To make matter's worse, my phone's battery died.

I *thought* I knew by heart my way to Amir's. Yet, the streets were unrecognizable that night. The roads were empty, and the shops were closed.

I made a series of wrong turns and stumbled upon a taxi kiosk. I pierced through the glass and spotted an old man ("the Old Man"). Desperate for a battery charger, I knocked on his window. He took one good look at me. The Old Man especially noticed my scuffed jeans, messy hair, and untied shoe laces. My pathetic imagery was enough for this gentle soul to take pity and open his doors.

Right away, he offered me water. The Old Man *knew* that I was dying of thirst. My insides felt cracked and dry like the desert ground.

After that spectacle, he offered me Kosher pastrami. I graciously declined and desperately asked, "Do you have an iPhone charger?" He did not. Still worse, I vaguely remembered Amir's phone number.

Like a broken record, I counted familiar numbers out loud. The Old Man waited in anticipation. At the stroke of midnight, I screamed, "Got it!" I grabbed his house phone and dialed the magic numbers. It rang forever. Just when I lost heart and settled for the pastrami, Amir answered!

I cried that precious moment when I heard his sweet voice. Before I could explain my whereabouts, a power outage hit the city. The phone line cut off, and the streets turned pitch-black.

I sat in the dark beside my dead phone eating pastrami with the Old Man.

One long hour passed, and systematically every other street lamp came to life.

The Old Man saw him before I did. He pointed his finger to the window, and my eyes followed. There stood Amir.

It was like my favorite scene from *Sixteen Candles*. After her sister's wedding, Samantha Baker stepped outside. The cars pulled away. That awesome song began. Jake Ryan stood by his Red Porsche, and they met halfway.

Like the incredulous Samantha Baker, I asked, "How did you know I was here?" He said, "I just knew."

At that moment and moments before, I also "just knew" he was the one. It was *always* Amir.

We said *"shalom"* ("goodbye" in Hebrew) to the Old Man, and Amir walked me home. Late that night, Amir went to the Penguin and found Eli. They had a "chat" about the status of my money, and lo and behold my money reappeared not a shekel short.

The Girl and Her Mattress

I needed a mattress for my bed, and my boss's wife, Yael, in a snub-nosed way pushed, *"Yasmeen. Rak, Dr. Gav"* ("Jasmine. Only Dr. Gav." in Hebrew). She had exquisite taste, and Dr. Gav was the Rolls Royce of Israeli mattresses.

I opted to be frugal and marched south to Herzl Street for a cheap deal.

I paced down 30 blocks and entered every store. Sidewalks were jam-packed with cushions and box springs. Merchants behaved like hot-blooded macho tough guys. Yet, I stayed in charge and tested each mattress meticulously. Sadly, my Italian boots gave in, and I hiked up empty-handed. Before long, Yael's sagacious advice came to light.

Tiny drizzles sprinkled on my face, and I looked up at the grey sky. Ten feet above me hung a bright red neon sign that flashed: "Dr. Gav." I pranced in ready to succumb to the wrath of retail.

Mordecai took his time and graciously offered me Turkish tea. His father, Eitan, behaved more aloof. Father and son wore *kippots* (caps worn by religious Jewish men at all times) and thick socks with Birkenstocks. By all means, they dressed humble and looked honest.

I accepted the refreshment and gazed at Mordecai. He popped a sugar cube in the center of his tongue and gulped the scorching tea. His glass was tulip-shaped. Like a pro, he expertly held it by the rim and saved his fingertips from being burned.

In an innocent lamblike tone, he asked, "What else can I offer?" I surrendered to him and replied, "I need a mattress." He spread his arms wide and said, "We have a wonderful selection."

I chose Dr. Gav's "Custom Comfort, All Natural Memory Foam" mattress. The price was a steal!

The next day, I returned with my Israeli cousin, Shaii. He was a Commander in the Israeli army and built like a Greek God. Shaii arrived dressed in uniform displaying his heroic badges.

This time, Mordecai served tea and *babka* (sweet Russian braided bread). Shaii savored every bite. He laughed at Mordecai's Israeli joke, and with his mouth full he mumbled, "They are honest." I paid the whole sum and delivery fee. Right before we left, Yael sent a fervent warning: *"Take peek-cher!"* ("Take a picture!"). Shaii followed her orders.

The big day finally arrived! I greeted the wimpy truck driver, and we pushed the mattress through my narrow, short door. I ripped the plastic but only just and did a double-take. The label read "Islander" and not "Dr. Gav." The mattress smelled like mildew and was as hard as a rock.

I ran outside, and the driver had sped off. It was as if he *knew* this story.

I snapped a shot of the "Islander," and I texted Mordecai, Shaii's picture and mine.

He replied: "Sweetie, I made a mistake. Come to the store Monday." I naively believed him.

Seconds later, he texted: "Don't remove the cover."

Thus, I slept on a plastic-wrapped mattress for five sleepless nights. I tossed and turned like a wild beast in captivity. Each time, the plastic made a loud "crackle." Friction between my aching body and the synthetic coating generated desert heat so much so that I had sweat bullets and got Stage One pneumonia.

I updated Yael on my health and well-being, and she was livid! She yelled, *"At Ameri-ka-ee! Hem oseem od kom-beenah!"* ("You're American! They will trick you again!" in Hebrew). I rebutted, "Again?" I felt like a gullible celebrity on MTV's show *Punk'd*, where Hollywood stars fell prey to elaborate pranks as fodder for American humor. There I was having just spotted the hidden cameras, and Austin Kutcher jumped out of the bushes and screamed, "Punk'd!"

Yael's hands shook, and her teeth clenched, as saliva bubbles foamed at her mouth. I believed that she was on the verge of a heart attack when she began to limp. My story had shocked her conscience.

Yael demanded, "You must call Benny!" Benny was her brother-in-law. She asserted, "He's a smart lawyer." For her sake, I agreed.

Benny wore an oversized V-neck shirt and ripped jeans. He walked pigeon-toed and behaved clumsy.

Mordecai gave Benny tea, and Benny gave Mordecai a business card. It read: *"Benny Orech Ha Deen"* ("Benny the Lawyer" in Hebrew).

Mordecai explained, "Your mattress is gone." Disheartened, I looked at Benny. Blank faced, Benny looked at Mordecai. It was like the blind leading the blind.

Mordecai saw an opening and jumped right in. "You deserve better than Dr. Gav, sweetie."

He locked the front door and led us to a wall in the back. He nudged the center wall, and it slowly opened outwards. There, a hook dangled. He gave it a yank, and stairs flopped open one-by-one. We climbed up and entered the "secret attic." It housed European mattresses worthy of the Royal Family.

Mordecai dimmed the lights, kicked on the ventilator, and played soft wavy music. Benny and I were in sleep heaven, and I forgot about Dr. Gav.

After much needed rest and relaxation, I chose my dream bed. The Swiss Bliss, "Double-Sided, Longevity Mattress." It was a touch bouncier than Dr. Gav, yet equipped with a triple action cooling agent to help me stay cool and sleep longer.

It cost four times the price of my first purchase and worth every shekel. I paid the full price minus my original fee.

Once again, my big day arrived! It was late Friday afternoon, and there was not a soul in sight.

The truck driver and his friend were muscular Ukrainians. They unloaded my mattress on the empty sidewalk, and I stopped them dead in their tracks. I couldn't believe my eyes! The label read "Dream Time" and not "Swiss Bliss."

Mordecai ignored my millions of calls, and I screamed, "I can't accept!" The bald Ukrainian grabbed my wrist and scolded, "You must!" Two against one, I had to accept the delivery.

They swapped the old with the new. Thankfully, my sofa (from another vendor) was already delivered, and I slept on that while Mordecai's creepy mattress rested in my bedroom.

My American credit card company remained one-sided. "Unfortunately Miss Jasmine, you accepted." I cried to the Indian operator and begged him for mercy. "Outlaws held me at gunpoint! I had to surrender!" He stuck to protocol for fear of deviating from the prescreened lines that he had memorized at his call center in Mumbai.

Mordecai believed in his own lies and repeated, "It's the same mattress, sweetie." My customary soft-spoken demeanor quickly skyrocketed into true Israeli rage, and I yelled, "I will sue you!" My blood boiled to insurmountable temperatures. I envisioned bribing a posse of Eritrean derelicts to defecate before the store that night and set it ablaze.

Like the operator, Mordecai didn't mind. He also knew about the "protocol" and gave me a ruthless deadline. "You must deliver in one day."

I felt defeated and weak. *How do I get a delivery truck? How much will it cost?*

My Zionist dreams of building a bigger and better Israel were shattered. *How can a Jew go against a Jew?* I naively believed that it was *us* against *them*.

My Yemenite Jewish neighbor, Amos, gave me hope.

Amos's skin was darker than charcoal, and his nose was bigger than a parrot's beak. He was a chain smoker, and his lips were chapped and purple. He was as thin as a rake, but very strong.

He heard my cries and offered me a Marlboro Red. I shared Every. Single. Detail. After, he clapped his hands and rejoiced, *"Yalla habibi!"* ("All right darling!" in Arabic). In anticipation, I rubbed my eyes and looked up at him. He vowed, "I know some guys," in the way a Jersey Shore Italian would "know some guys" with particular skills at dismantling kneecaps.

The day arrived. Amos and I waited long outside my apartment. My stomach turned in circles, and my ears rang. I felt defeated.

Teary-eyed, I begged him, "Amos where is your friend?" He said nothing and remained calm.

At 2:33 p.m., a larger than life pick-up truck arrived. Two short Serbians jumped out and flew past me. They swiftly carried and loaded the mattress onto the truck's bed (back of the truck). In a single hop, they jumped on and faced each other. Like Western cowboys, they twirled their lassos and caught opposite corners of the mattress. They jerked the rope and secured the cargo. At full-speed, they cartwheeled across the truck's bed.

Of course, they finished with a triple axel jump and landed on both feet. The hairy one glided to the driver's seat, and the other opened the passenger's side. He gestured, "lady's first," and I skipped right in. In half a second, he leaped in, and we sped off!

En route, I sat with a Serb on my lap, and Amos followed in a dilapidated scooter. We arrived in the nick of time.

For the first time, I noticed a suspicious subtlety. Directly 20 feet above their "Dr. Gav" sign, hung another! In tiny letters it read: *"Aloof Ha Meezroneem, Baam 1998"* ("Champion of Mattresses, Est. 1998" in Hebrew). By day they posed as "Dr. Gav," but were nothing short of snake oil salesmen touting a cure that was worse than the disease!

This round, Mordecai kept quiet, and Eitan spoke. He besieged me with insults! He pointed his finger and shouted, *"Hee Sah-tan!"* ("She's Satan!" in Hebrew). Amos heard enough and yelled, *"Maspeek! Maspeek!"* ("Enough! Enough!" in Hebrew).

I gently placed my hand on Amos's chest to *tell* him, "I got this." I stared into Eitan's ugly eyes and defended my honor. I shouted, *"Ani haseeyut shel ha Sah-tan!"* ("I'm Satan's worst nightmare!" in Hebrew).

They begrudgingly accepted their phony Swiss Bliss and returned my money.

For several nights, I slept on my sofa. In the dusk of dawn, I spotted a gigantic madman behind my balcony.

He repeatedly pounded the glass door. My heart raced, and my body froze. Our eyes locked, and he stared at me on and on. After endless attempts, he put his head down and drifted into the darkness.

I slept with my eyes wide open and dreamt that he beat me to death. With his bare hands, he tore open my chest cavity and ripped out my organs. Then, he sold them for pennies to Uzbekistan's black market. I was a missing person. Actually, no one even knew that I was dead for days then weeks. Until, greedy Tzvika saw that his rent money was short. Then again, I had paid him four months in advance because he didn't trust Americans. Thus, it would be months until someone realized that I was gone. By then, I dreamt that the Israeli cockroaches would have nibbled and swallowed thick chunks of my rotten, smelly flesh.

That morning, I rushed to Amos and recounted my near-death experience. He sprinted to the open terrace that was located behind our building. There, stood a wooden ladder that led directly to my balcony! Amos violently pulled it down and crushed it to pieces.

He ran to his apartment, and like a pack of wolves I followed. Amos was so quick that he had already left and waited outside of mine. With incredible finesse, he led me in and skillfully installed a double lock. The calm after the storm finally settled, and hindsight is truly 20/20.

But for Eitan and Mordecai's tricks, I would have never slept on my couch, seen my perpetrator, discovered the ladder, and installed a safety lock. Somewhere inside my shattered heart, I thanked them for saving my life. Also, I blessed Amos.

Three years later, Mordecai and Eitan were caught stealing red-handed. The video debuted, and karma was the Devil waiting for them in the ring. A disgruntled pro-wrestler recognized Mordecai and Eitan and beheaded them underneath their neon Dr. Gav sign.

One may say, Mordecai and Eitan are villains. Equally, they were the rotten seeds on a beautiful grapevine called "Eretz Israel."

Devil "Who Thinks" He Wears Prada

I first met them at a candlelight dinner. They donned Hawaiian polos and sat tall. Boaz was leggy, and Arik was short. I pictured Arnold Schwarzenegger and Danny Devito in the movie *Twins*. Their skin glowed in the dark, and their fake teeth sparkled. They were Tel Aviv gays and fabulous.

Boaz and Arik shared everything-a bed, a business, and much more. They were the dynamic duo behind Klein Wedding Couture. Boaz was the designer extraordinaire, and Arik was the charlatan.

Instantly, we formed a bond over vogue, sexy men, and French pastry. Four months had passed, and I quit my job as a tax attorney. They heard the news and hired me at once.

I spearheaded international sales and was held captive by their beautiful and illustrious gowns. It was my dream come true until day three when Arik's light-hearted facade was tragically unveiled.

It was after lunch, and I was alone with Arik and his assistant, Vanessa, when a Greek retailer reneged on an order. Arik wore high-heeled high tops and screamed in a frenzy, *"Ha-lach ha kesef!"* ("My money is gone!" in Hebrew). Then he cried like a baby. Best of all, he threw his shoe at the scared wall.

Finally, I heard dead silence. That moment, a bright-eyed bride-to-be entered and noticeably held 7,000 Shekels. With one shoe, Arik limped and gave her a great, big hug.

Vanessa strutted next door and ordered an iced-cappuccino. She inserted her index finger before the flamboyant clerk's face and gave him a come-hither motion. Oddly, he leaned over, and she whispered in his ear, *"Bah la bayit"* ("On the house" in Hebrew). Every day, she coaxed the spineless fool to put her coffee on Arik's tab.

Vanessa was poor and acted rich. She posed as an international celebrity and bragged, "You know. I have *beeeg* ("big") connection in Hollywood." I pretended to nod.

The clerk was lanky, and his oval head wobbled. He was madly in love with Boaz and despised Arik with a passion. He worked for a concept store that was owned by a fancy French woman who envied Klein Couture's massive success.

Arik's meeting with the bride was *chik chak* ("quick" in Hebrew slang). He promised her a Cinderella dress and a veil that's hand-embroidered in Swarovski crystals. She believed his every word. He quickly pocketed the dough and rushed her out.

Arik hurled an evil laugh and blasted Alabina's infamous "Habibi" ("Alabina" is an Israeli music group). He spread his arms, lifted his head, and twirled like a fairy. He circled on his tippy-toes toward Vanessa, and still with one shoe they sexually belly-danced. For now, he was happy, and I was tone-deaf and terrified.

Day 8. I heard voices in the basement.

Day 12. The bright-eyed bride had her first fitting, and there was no dress to be fitted. Arik showed her used dresses, and Vanessa modeled.

Horrified, the bride screamed at the top of her lungs. Of course, Arik yelled back, *"Aval mami! Zeh style!"* ("But sweetie! This is style!" in Hebrew). She wept hysterically and ran out.

Day 13. The bride returned with her fiancé, who wore a tracksuit and a chunky gold watch. Arik casually said, "Hey." The fiancé clenched his pocketknife, and I saw its sharp tip. Vanessa anxiously hovered behind Arik, but really she towered over him. Arik zipped open a zebra striped leather pouch and gave me exact cash. I handed it over, feeling scared to death, and the young couple left.

Arik let out air, and wiped the sweat off of his forehead with his middle finger. He screamed, *"Ay-foh ha moo-zee-kah!"* ("Where is the music!" in Hebrew). In a flash, Shakira's "My Hips Don't Lie" played. ("Shakira" is a Columbian singer.)

He shook his pelvis like an Israeli Elvis. Vanessa went wild and yelled, *"Od!" "Od!"* ("More!" "More!" in Hebrew). He stripped off his silk cami and beat his chest like Tarzan.

Vanessa kneeled on all fours, and Arik jumped on her tail. He rode her like a black stallion. Their bodies merged and became half-human, half-horse just like the Centaur in Greek mythology.

They galloped away to the concept store, and Vanessa ate *bourekas* (Israeli pastry) "on the house."

Day 15. It was before 8 a.m., and I was alone or so I thought. I heard voices in the basement, and I daringly crept down.

The basement was strictly prohibited, and curiosity got the best of me. I took my last step and stumbled upon a door. I opened it, and the chit chat was loud and clear. There, sat 12 Russian seamstresses. The air was thick and sweaty. They had dark eyes, and their fingertips were pointy and hardened from their endless toil of sharp needles and no rest.

Appalled, I ran up speechless from the flagrant abuse of labor laws in the Promised Land.

Day 21. Arik dramatically opened the armoire and slammed it shut. He shrieked, *"Ay-foh ha kubeh!"* ("Where is my kubeh!" in Hebrew) ("Kubeh" is an Israeli meat dumpling).

From the corner of his hungry eye, he gnarled at a bride's *babi* ("Grandmother" in Yiddish). Arik grabbed her purse, and she held on tight. They played tug and war until she dropped and broke her hip.

That morning, I entered the dressing room and saw Vanessa inhaling kubeh. Caught red-handed, she bent her claws like an angry cheetah and made a "hissed" sound. I picked up the dresses and ran away.

Babi was carried away in a stretcher, and Arik acted dead from starvation. Vanessa gave him mouth-to-mouth, and magically he came back to life.

First things first, he eyeballed me and screamed, *"Yasmeen! At shmeh-nah!"* ("Jasmine, you are fat!" in Hebrew). I said nothing about everything.

Day 22. I arrived at a quarter past 9 a.m. Arik sat with Vanessa and yelled, "Yasmeen! You are late!" I turned around and left. Two hours later, he texted: "My heart miss you!" I shunned his weak attempts to assuage me.

A week earlier, Arik and Boaz had purchased a computer. I had transferred files from my laptop onto a DiscOnKey, and from there to the computer. Unbeknownst to me, the night before I quit, Arik and Boaz returned that computer, and they foolishly made no backup.

By late afternoon, Arik demanded my laptop. He burst: "Your computer is mine!" I ignored him, and his text screamed back: "I will report you to the Police! You are *chutzpanit!*" (derogatory term in Hebrew for women who exhibit nerve).

They owed me a commission, and in return, I agreed to give them the DiscOnKey. Oddly, we met inside the basement, and I saw the indentured Russians one last time. They took my DiscOnKey and promised to pay me the first of the month. Of course, they never did.

The story did not end there. Karma came swiftly and paid Arik a sweet visit. He and Boaz broke up, and Arik lost his business.

But wait, it gets juicier. Arik was entangled in tumultuous love affairs with Asian mafia gangsters. One in particular was named "Thai Man."

You see, Thai Man was an extremely jealous lover. He framed Arik in the heat of passion. Arik was caught with his pants down (literally) and 50 kilos of cocaine. He served a life sentence in a Thai prison, scarier than Alcatraz. One day, he got bit by a monkey and died. Finally, the end.

"Does this belong to you?"

Pandora's Box

I was blessed with good luck to have celebrated Shabbat with Amir and his parents.

My favorite moments were when Amir's father placed his hands on Amir's head and sang a timeless wish for Hashem's guidance and protection that's been recited for 3,000 years by Jewish fathers.

At times, he whispered a "secret blessing" to his daughter and sons-a trait that he admired about his child, or a funny story that they shared.

The blessing was sealed with a lasting hug, and it was at that moment that I realized that I missed my father more than ever before.

In the same way, his mother's exquisite tablescape charmed every guest.

Amir's mother, Daphne, decorated her table with white daffodils in a blue vase at its center to glorify the beauty of God's creations: a glass oil lamp that emitted light in the midst of darkness, a silver goblet to celebrate the splendor of Shabbat through the power of wine, and a silk *challah* (braided Shabbat bread) cover that was embroidered with Jerusalem's Old City Walls in a sea of vibrant shades. Upon my arrival, she invited me to light the Shabbat candles, which was her finishing touch to the magnificent tablescape that made me feel special.

My heart knew that I was ready to honor these traditions with a family of my own.

One Friday night, in June of 2016, it was a quintessential Shabbat until Daphne opened Pandora's Box.

She asked Amir, "What are your intentions with Yasmeen?"
Amir confessed, "I'm not ready for wedding bells."
Daphne said, "Then, you must set her free."
Amir alleged, "What's a piece of paper when love exists?"
Daphne declared, "Love is a fantasy without a written promise."
Amir swore, "But, I vow to cherish her!"
Daphne implored, "Then, take a giant leap of faith!"

It was my turn to take the floor, but I remained complaisant because love had blinded me.

One day later, Amir conceded to me, "My mom is right." I closed the door of his car after I cried farewell to him forever. Step by step, I broke free from the past through forgiveness-accepting the present by creating new memories; and looking forward to the future because I walked with faith.

"Clap your Hands"

In July, my girlfriend from Los Angeles, Celine, arrived to Tel Aviv for holiday. Of course, I was brokenhearted, and our summer shenanigans were just what the doctor had ordered.

One Thursday night, we painted the town red at the Shalvata Beach Club ("Shalvata" or "beach club") that was once an old hangar ("the old hangar") in the Namal (Tel Aviv Port), and the very spot that Amir and I had first met.

The line to get into the Shalvata stretched longer than the Great Wall of China. Thus, I edged my way through the crowd to the top and bamboozled the host to roll out the red carpet for us because I posed as an American Reality Star from the faux docudrama, *Beverly Hills Gold Diggers*.

The beach club was bustling with thousands. We squeezed our way elbow-to-elbow to the ring-shaped bar at the center of the Shalvata to refresh and recharge from our dramatic entrance.

I shook off the sand pebbles that had slid in my peep-toe espadrilles when I glanced up and laid eyes on him face-to-face!

In my mind, the heart-pounding music softened, and the bright lights dimmed. Then, a spotlight captured us.

That's when, I tapped his shoulder and said, "Amir?" with a cheeky smile. He stared up from his screen, and his eyes caught mine. Instantaneously, I blushed, and my heart skipped a beat. I felt butterflies fluttering in my stomach.

He stared speechlessly with his eyebrows half-raised; his eyes wide open; and, his lips half-parted.

Amir popped up out of thin air and amid thousands! I pondered, *What were the odds?*

A moment later, he said, "Hi." Just then, the disc jockey ("D.J. Asher" or "D.J.") played "Clap your Hands" ("the song") by D.J. Solomun. The song tells us to clap our hands, stomp our feet, and feel the love as we dance. The warm sea breeze ruffled my hair, and I was ready to spin the night away in his arms.

The fusion of the sun-kissed vibes of the Shalvata, the backdrop of the Mediterranean Sea, and the hottest hit that rocked our bodies cautioned and confused Amir, as he mouthed, "Goodbye."

The music grew louder, and the spotlight vanished. Only the scent of the warm sand beneath my feet lingered from our chance meeting; and Celine wiped away my tears. She shouted at the top of her voice and bet her bottom dollar that he'll return *after* this wild Israeli summer.

I heard her Celine loud and clear, yet D.J. Solomun's hypnotic melody struck a chord that shot a sudden chill down my spine, and suddenly her promise felt superfluous.

I had lost my courage momentarily at a spontaneous chance with love and regained my courage back. The very courage that had uplifted me after a broken heart and had emboldened me to blaze away to Israel and empowered me to stay despite the *balagan*! ("Balagan" is "chaos" in Hebrew.)

Thus, I pulled myself up by the bootstraps, danced, stamped my feet, and felt the love as I danced the night away by myself and my broken heart since courage and love go hand in hand.

If the Shoe Fits

Despite this bump in the road, Celine and I had the time of our lives at the Shalvata, and she begged me to take her back. Thus, one week later, we set off to the Shalvata in a shirut for a night out on the town to send Celine off in style!

I was dressed to kill in a baby blue, A-line dress with a sweeping skirt and a tight bodice that cinched at my waistline. I dolled up in a velvet black choker and wore a silver Fendi Baguette (designer handbag) as a status symbol. My "glass" slippers that had a crystal bowtie at the front were the crowning jewel to my fairytale look.

We were packed like a can of sardines inside the shirut that had been burning fuel since 1948 and was on its last legs.

A Filipino caregiver crushed my big toe as he sidled up next to me and mumbled, "Shalom," in his shy voice.

The little room inside the minivan spawned more intimacy than the unisex steam room at the Gordon Gym, yet I never let it cramp my style.

Thus, before the clock struck midnight, I slipped my glass slipper back on and pranced down the rickety steps of the shirut feeling whimsical, dreamy, and passionate like Cinderella when she graced the ballroom at the royal ball and charmed the knickers off Prince Charming.

Upon our arrival to the Shalvata, I laid eyes on "Roman the Romanian" ("Roman"). He was a far cry from Prince Charming.

Roman the Romanian was the hired gun at the Shalvata and selected to protect us from the bad guys. The "bad guys" are Arab and Palestinian terrorists who aim to massacre Jews in cold blood.

He had giant muscles, fluffy black hair, droopy eyes, and a slurred speech. Roman displayed a classic Manhattan Fedora hat to radiate power. He donned a pair of fingerless black gloves to help him grip his pistol and to pull the trigger with tactile precision.

Roman the Romanian's well-fitted jeans and laced-up leather army boots exposed his no-nonsense approach to fashion while defending Jewish lives.

He buffed his silver ring against his cotton shirt to polish the olive tree, with its deep roots, that was etched on the shiny metal and is the symbol of the 1st "Golani" Brigade-an elite combat unit of the Israel Defense Forces.

Roman spent his childhood in an orphanage in Romania devoid of laughter and play. After, he made *Aliyah* ("Immigration to Israel" in Hebrew) as a lone soldier to be all that he can be in the army. I knew this because Amir had saved his life when he had pulled the trigger first on the battlefield.

He patted us down from head to toe in case anyone had on a clandestine suicide vest, and he didn't break a sweat in his off-the-rack, classic Italian leather jacket.

Despite the tough reality of living in Israel, I never let it break my spirit because that's when the bad guys will win.

Roman the Romanian, or shall I say "Rocky Balboa," pointed his baton to the end of the line.

Celine is as American as apple pie and chased herself to the end of the road! Since, she plays by the rules, I pulled out all the stops to stop her. I'm a Persian Jew, and we never wait in line!

The eyewitness testimony from an Ashkenazi bride ("the Bride") who took a bizarre spin to Eskandar's Kosher Grocery Store ("Eskandar's") in Los Angeles is the proof in the pudding. ("Ashkenazi Jews" came from Central or Eastern Europe, and most Jews in America are Ashkenazi.)

Picture this, she's in a long line that stretched farther than the eye can see at Eskandar's and is greeted by Persian Hip-Hop music that's played by a loudspeaker that's about to collapse on someone's head.

The songs have an energetic beat and poetic lyrics that rhyme about true love. Momentarily, the bride daydreams about her husband because she's mad about him. Suddenly, she is shaken awake by a true nightmare and sees that her life is in danger.

One Persian Jewish grandmother (*"Mamanbozorg"* in Farsi) rammed her carry cruiser that had wheels of steel and was designed to tackle any terrain against the heels of the bride because she believed that her carry cruiser was a Rolls Royce, and she never stepped on the brakes when she made a sharp turn into the exotic spice lane at lightning speed.

Eskandar's is scattered with the ruins of tinned cans that had no price tag, and regretful brides believe that these "delicacies" at Eskandar's are priceless and so is the experience! But, I dare digress.

The Bride's gash led a bloody trail to the frozen foods lane where "Notary by Jamshid" gives his stamp of approval that nobody had asked for, as he stood behind a children's lemonade stand.

The bride turns around to confront her perpetrator and collapses onto the cold granite because she lost a pint of blood. Mamanbozorg warns the unconscious bride, "No one cry at Eskandar's!" and then pointed to her shin guards that she donned underneath her mamanbozorg frock.

Swiftly, a different mamanbozorg careens her carry cruiser with supersonic speed and proceeds to pillage the Bride's produce. She and Mamanbozorg were partners in crime! The grumpy cashier screams, "Yalla!," and the regulars step on the Bride and advance to the front.

Notary by Jamshid holds sumac, an ancient Persian spice with a strong citrus scent, below the Bride's nose to bring her back to life because she was shoeless, braw-less, soulless, hairless, penniless, toothless, spineless, humorless, clueless, mindless, nameless, hopeless, helpless, useless, breathless, defenseless, voiceless, worthless, fatherless, motherless, and sadly, spice-less beneath the loud speaker that was about to collapse on her head.

I couldn't let that happen to me that night at the Shalvata!

My ancestors had mastered the skill of survival inside the *mahaleh's* (Jewish ghettos in Iran), and I had fallen heir to their wisdom.

Roman the Romanian clicked on his tally counter for fun because he was a on a power trip as the gatekeeper to the Shalvata. The young women who he had rejected with the flick of a thumb of a Roman emperor, flung themselves at his feet and opened their wallets since they had tried every trick in the book. He aired a stiff upper lip. I reckon that long queues were common to Roman the Romanian who was born and bred under communism; and he couldn't shake off the weight of the old hammer and sickle.

I pondered, *Can I turn this into a game of Football?* I held my Fendi against my chest and barreled through the line. I elbowed and tackled hundreds to live it up at the Shalvata. Then, I leaped over the velvet red rope and slam dunked my Fendi onto the concrete floor and proclaimed, "Who's in charge now Roman!" Roman's jaw dropped, and I breezed into the Shalvata as a V.I.P.-a "Very Important Persian."

Well, not exactly.

Precisely then, a gaggle of beautiful Israeli twentysomethings ("the beautiful girls") hopped out of a red Jeep and soared across the old hangar from a zip line because Israelis love excitement.

One by one, the beautiful girls jumped down from high above the Shalvata and landed on both feet! The voice in the back of my head screamed, *Holy Moses! They intercepted my touchdown!* Suddenly, I had to switch plays.

The beautiful girls spun themselves in a circle, and their long hair fell down from their ponytails. I remembered with excitement the iconic spin that had transformed Diana Prince into Wonder Woman.

They flipped, twirled, spun, and tossed their beautiful hair to the sea, sky, and land. I scuttled to them as fast as my legs would carry me and flipped, twirled, spun, and tossed my curly hair until I felt that my neck was about to break.

With my neck remarkably intact, I asked one, "Do you need a light?" and she leaned forward with a cigarette in her mouth. The red label warning on her Capri Slims put an ugly face to the beautiful girl's bad habit, and just like that, I lit their fires with a vintage matchbox of a 1950's pin-up girl, who was photographed in a one-piece swimsuit with platinum blonde hair, red lips, and a playful over-the-shoulder smile, that I had taken from Amir's bedside drawer.

All of my life, I had prayed for this moment! It was like my favorite scene from *Mean Girls*. Cady Heron mustered her courage to sit with The Plastics, who were teen royalty, at their lunch table. Then, Regina George, the leader of the Plastics, tells Cady Heron that she's really pretty. Like the courageous Cady Heron, I mingled with Israeli royalty at the Shalvata!

It was a far cry from the day that I had squeezed myself into the candy-apple-red leather pants or into the inflatable ball gown to impress Suzy, Stacey, Mrs. Berger, Rabbi Gooz, Coach, the jocks, the cool girls who had boyfriends, the teachers' pets, the nerds, the loners, the deviants, the Kosher chef, the nurse, the librarians, the crossing guard, the bus drivers, the janitors, and anyone with two eyes and a heartbeat at my Jewish day school.

I stared at Roman as he continued to usher in the beautiful girls, and his ice-cold eyes tested my courage! Since, it takes chutzpah to pull a fast one on Roman!

I affixed myself to them like glue and slipped past Roman amid their clouds of smoke, as I choked to death. I entered the Shalvata closer to death than the woman in the 1997 anti-tobacco campaign who smoked from a hole in her throat.

Immediately, the beautiful girls were whisked away by rich men who liked to spend money on booze, and I dragged my heels to an empty stool. My hair and skin stank of nicotine, acetone, arsenic, formaldehyde, benzene, butane, carbon monoxide, hydrogen cyanide, and radioactive chemicals that could lead to me growing a tail!

On my way, I saw bottles of *arak* ("arak" is a licorice-flavored liquor that originated in the Middle-East and has 40%-80% alcohol content) floating on a sheet of water at the bar top that was made from aircraft aluminum. Suddenly, I ran the like the Road Runner in *Looney Tunes* who was never eaten by the Coyote, and I suffered blows, cuts, and jabs. The courage that lived on inside of me vowed, *For I have seen better days and this too shall pass!* At last, I arrived to the empty stool, and it was on its last legs! I prayed, *Dear God, please watch over me tonight.*

Surprisingly, the bottles of arak that I had seen floating on water had vanished, and they seemed unbelievably real. I ordered from the bartender a triple and said to him, "I can handle the truth. Give it to me straight up!" I knocked back a shot in one gulp, grimaced, and ordered a second, a third, and another.

The arak warmed my body from head to toe and erased from my memory all traces of smoke inhalation *and* whiplash. I felt invincible because I was intoxicated with confidence.

The crowd was cliquey and deliriously wild. At the bar, the Jewish Brits ("the Brits") drank like fish and danced together decidedly wasted, all the while carving out their turf in the Shalvata because they will stumble out and return tomorrow.

The young chaps were likeable and charming in their baggy denims, spiky gelled-up hair, long sleeve rugby polo shirts in navy blue and green stripes, and oversized flannel shirts that were often tied around the waist. Their sweethearts dressed loud in sky-high platforms, hot-pink baby doll dresses, bright-blue jumpsuits, purple sequined frocks that were barely-there, pig tails, floral hair barrettes, and metallic eyeshadow.

The Brits showed their true colors with their touch of prep; hint of grunge; and show of sparkles because they felt at home in Eretz Israel.

I was the fly on the wall and felt as if I was spying on a live taping of an Ambercombie & Fitch commercial, in the 90's, featuring Kurt Cobaine doppelgängers and the Spice Girls. The night was moving faster than a silent movie. I tried to stay present in the moment and all of a sudden, the Frenchies ("French Jews") caught my eye.

Roman escorted them to white couches and white end tables that were front and center at the Shalvata. Right there, I read: "V.I.P." on a stand alone neon sign and had a sinking feeling that I was unwelcome.

They were assigned private cocktail girls to help them pour their Dom Pérignon into their champagne flutes, to light their cigarettes, to cool their ice, to take their pictures, to fluff their pillows, to wipe their mouths, to shine their shoes, and massage their feet because the French love to feel like royalty at Versailles.

They were deeply tanned and matched in white linen from top to bottom.

Quickly, I caught onto their ways. One young woman gazed at other men lustfully. Naturally, they gazed back at her. Then, she rolled her eyes to "tell" them "beat it!" That's when they sheepishly looked away, and she knew that she had played them like a fiddle.

On-the-spot, the cocktail girls held up champagne bottles that were lit by sparklers that had sparks higher than seven inches to add more spark to the night, and I felt a sudden tap on my shoulder. Holy mackerel, it was Celine!

I asked, "Did you sneak in?" and she replied, "Do nice girls finish last?" with a cheeky grin. Her answer was a baffling mystery, and I was onto to her! Thus, I asked, "Then, where was Roman?" Celine shrugged her shoulders, acting clueless.

Wait a minute! Stop right there! Hold your horses! The voice in my head screamed, *Who are you, and what have you done with my goody-two shoes, play-by-the book, afraid of her own shadow, and scared of the dark friend, Celine!*

I tossed back a shot of arak, confident that I can solve this baffling mystery. I was close, but no cigar.

In hindsight, Roman, the beautiful girls, the bartender, the Brits, the Frenchies, the cocktail girls, the bad guys, and *moi* had rubbed off on Celine. Since, Israel is truly the Wild, Wild West of the Middle East!

In haste, D.J. Asher turned up the volume, exponentially. *Did he have a late-night gig?* Everyone stopped in their tracks when they heard the deep house remix of *Hava Nagila* (Jewish folk song) and stormed the dance floor in the same fashion as the Israelites who stormed the Red Sea before its waves came crashing down onto the Egyptian army. I lost a shoe on the way, as I'm sure many Israelite women did.

The buzz that swept over us intensified, and we danced together, after 2,700 years of exile, to deep house music as one gigantic *mishpacha* ("Family" in Hebrew).

On the dance floor, the beautiful girls and the even more beautiful Israeli girls electrified us with their supernatural beauty. They donned blue denims, ripped at the knee, and loose-fitting tees. Their smiles were their best and only makeup.

Celine held my hand, and we danced the *Hora* (Jewish circle dance) to the Hava Nagila with our Jewish brothers and Jewish sisters at lightning speed. I got stepped on, punched, shoved, and clobbered and cherished every scab, bruise, and wound that I had sustained because the Hora embodied the Jewish people's expression of happiness and unity.

The beautiful girls and the other beautiful Israeli girls had formed a smaller circle inside of ours and stayed cool because they were *Sabras*. ("Sabra" is the Hebrew name for the Prickly Pear Cactus and a nickname for Israeli Jews who were born in Israel.) Like the Sabra plant, they were tough on the outside and soft and sweet on the inside.

The Hava Nagila was ending fast, and D.J. Asher glanced down at us from high above his stage that shook wildly beneath his feet. We glanced back up at him and had hope in our eyes, love in our hearts, and spirit in our souls. This, in essence, is the power of *Am Israel* or the People of Israel.

Suddenly, the music stopped and D.J. Asher chanted on his microphone, *"Am Israel Chai!"* ("The People of Israel Live!" in Hebrew). He raised his arms up and down, motioning us to chant louder than him. Like a fiddler on the roof, D.J. Asher spun wild tunes and led us from one Jewish dance tune to another all night long.

Celine grabbed my hand and drove us through the dance floor that was bursting at the seams. Fired-up and coordinated, she hopped up on stage with a bang!

She extended her arm toward the crowd and then moved her hand toward herself to taunt the bad guys, "Bring it!" because she was a proud Jew at last. Celine screamed at the top of her lungs, "I am not a Jew with trembling knees!" echoing Israeli Prime Minister, Menachem Begin.

I jumped up, and my hands gripped the edge of the stage for dear life as the tiny pieces of wood dug into my skin. *Is this what living on the edge looks like?* My fingers bled and turned black and blue. I glanced down, and my legs dangled in the air since they had nowhere to go. Right then, I air-kicked a go-go dancer in the face.

My fear of getting in hot water with Roman was the catapult that propelled me to centerstage with one shoe and in dire need of medical attention.

I crawled to Celine who was raising the roof with D.J. Asher inside the D.J. booth, and all that I could see was thick, billowing smoke that blasted me at turbo speed from the jets, staged at close range, because Israelis love special effects.

My body flung to the four corners of the earth, and that was just the tip of the iceberg. The thick, billowing "smoke" was dry ice better known as Carbon Dioxide. Moments later, I sustained frostbite, nerve injuries, confusion, and mild to severe asphyxiation. I wondered, *Dear God, are you watching over me tonight?*

Celine came to my rescue wearing a gas mask that belonged to D.J. Asher because who knows when the bad guys will strike?

She dragged me by the arms to the D.J. booth that had four protective panels, and we made it just in the nick of time because the jets had gone haywire. I imagined that the bad guys had hijacked the jets and fired them in every direction from their shoulders like a bazooka.

Inside, my eardrums were about to burst from D.J. Asher's earsplitting beats, and time hung at a standstill. Indeed, I wore a gas mask, yet tragically I discovered that a gas mask protects one against gas and not smoke. Hence the name!

Between short, rapid breaths, I had bet that Roman, the beautiful girls, the bartender, the Brits, the Frenchies, and the cocktail girls reveled in the revelry because they returned night after night.

I thought that I had seen everything under the sun, and that's when the confetti show and the laser light show erupted. I pondered, *Dear God, when will this three-ring circus end?*

I was buried in confetti and could only see out of my left eye. I looked like a wet chicken that stood idle in a six-lane highway.

Celine shouted from D.J. Asher's silver mic, "Let the good times roll!" and she did! Thus, I took one for the team and stayed put for endless hours until sunrise.

After the smoke show, the laser light show, and the confetti show, that had confetti magically fall from heaven like manna, I clawed my way up.

The sky was bright orange and yellow. Its bright colors illuminated the crescent moon.

I slumped over the side panels and began to count the number of days that I had left in this world.

I stared straight ahead, and a silhouette emerged from the shroud of smoke, seemingly walking on air. I had a funny feeling in my bones. The silhouette looked manly. *Who can he be?*

He walked with confidence and kept his gaze up, walking ahead of everyone. I wiped the foggy lenses of my gas mask, and the silhouette was closer than it appeared because Amir was right in front of me.

Did he know that it was me behind the gas mask? Then, he said my name.

Amir removed my gas mask and tried to kiss me on the lips. Flustered, I pulled back. His skin glowed, and he smelled like the summer, floral and citrus scents. He kneeled, and like a magician, Amir opened his hand and revealed my lost shoe.

Like Prince Charming in *Cinderella*, Amir yearned to know which fair maiden's dainty foot would fit this glass slipper. I tried the shoe on, and it fit perfectly. Before I knew it, Amir vanished into the sunset *without me*.

I buried my pain and carried on with that funny feeling in the pit of my stomach.

One month later, on a Monday night in August, Amir sent me a text message: "Will you go on a date with me?" I pondered, *What could he want, now?*

The next day, we met at a bistro in Tel Aviv named, "Gourmet Sabzi." The Persian bistro was named after the Persian dish, "gormeh sabzi," and Amir asked with a smile, "Do you like the name?" I replied, staring deeply into his eyes, "Yes, deeply."

For a moment, my elbows stuck to the vinyl table cover that was embroidered in gold roses and silver leaves. We sat on his-and-her lawn chairs that had spaghetti straps on the seat and back and a cup-holder. Our table was dimly lit by one candle on a tin tray. The centerpiece was a topless, battery-operated Hawaiian Hula girl. I poked around, and her coconut bra was nowhere to be seen.

The table behind me had a Malibu Barbi and Ken centerpiece. The accent shelf displayed a terrified baby Buddha. A small fire burned above the mantel that had a headshot of Ayatollah Khomeini giving the bird from behind bars in a speedo. I stepped on a frosted Christmas tree because it was two feet high.

My head was spinning!

The owner, Davood, reclined upside down on his executive office chair that had six broken wheels and a retractable ottoman. I only saw his feet in the air. His wife, Yaffa, sat on a school chair that had a desk and cut *sabzi*. ("Sabzi" are fresh green herbs in Farsi.)

They blasted Persian radio from a boombox. I wondered where our waiter was. Right then, Davood shouted, "Today's special is ghormeh sabzi!"

Is ghormeh sabzi really today's special, or is it the only dish that's on the menu? Hence the name, "Gourmet Sabzi!" Amir shouted, "We'll have the special!" and broke the ice at our table.

In a snap, Yaffa served us ghormeh sabzi over Persian rice from a hot pot and donned a statement t-shirt that read: "Be my Valentines." I smelled sweet, pungent fenugreek. Our paper plates featured Dora the Explorer taking a bubble bath. I wondered, *Did Davood and Yaffa stop at a garage sale on their way to Israel from Iran?*

She threw at us plastic forks and spoons because Persians eat rice with a spoon. Yaffa shouted from the rooftops, "Nobody take knife at Gourmet Sabzi!"

Did Yaffa barter her good manners for trinkets at the garage sale? We laughed, and we laughed out loud. Manners are as useless in Israel as boobs on a nun.

The candle's flame blew out, and I pulled out Amir's matchbox from inside my Fendi. "Here, I'll light it," he said. I used my fork to push the rice into my spoon, still laughing. Then, he popped the question! Yaffa grabbed a seat even though Davood, who remained upside down, may have died from brain damage because his entire blood supply had rushed to his brain.

Amir asked again and again, "Will you be my girlfriend?" I returned his matchbox back inside my Fendi where it has remained ever since.

The Princess Diaries

The date was Friday, February 10, 2017, and I was running late because Shabbat was almost here.

A bitter cold had entered my bedroom through the bottom of my front door, and my furnace was working harder than an ugly stripper.

I hopped inside his Peugeot convertible, and Amir revved the engine with a grin on his face. *Vroom! Vroom!* the engine roared. Suddenly, he disengaged the clutch pedal and stepped on the gas!

My hair blew in the wind, tousled and curly. I blasted the radio and sang along to Israeli pop songs that I didn't know.

The highway had one lane in each direction and was divided by yellow rumble strips. Amir drove fast and took chances like an Italian race car driver. I was unafraid with him by my side.

Pretty soon, the arrow had touched the red zone. My curly hair flew everywhere. The wind began tugging the follicles on my head. *Is this what it means to live life in the fast lane?*

I was certain that I'd never have a bad hair day because the wind would pull the hair straight out of my head.

Amir soared toward a line of cars. I screamed, "Are you racing against time!" "Do you trust me?" he said confidently as he shifted from first gear to second gear smoother than a pro race car driver.

I saw my life, and the follicles on my head, flash before my eyes. Before I knew it, Amir had crossed over to the other side, and I felt from underneath my seat the yellow rumble strips.

"Look out!," I shrieked. A grey hatchback came barreling toward us, head-on! Amir said in hushed tones, "Timing is everything." *But, was there enough time?*

A moment later, he eased his right foot off the gas and pressed his left foot down on the clutch, softly and steadily. Right then, he gently pushed the gear lever from second to neutral and then to third. Instantaneously, he released the clutch and stepped on the gas, being smooth on the throttle! His hands and feet slowly danced together, back and forth, in perfect synchrony.

I kept my eyes open the entire time. The sunset was beating down on us, and the stretch at the end of the highway twisted and turned.

It was now or never! We flew toward the grey hatchback, and its driver, past his prime, flashed bright orange lights at us as if his life depended on it. Amir stayed in the zone, looking rapt and focused.

Suddenly, the bright orange lights hit Amir's eyes. The moment just before we were about to crash, I locked eyes with him across the way. His old face was as white as a ghost, covered with wrinkles and frozen with fear.

Then, it was about to happen; I gasped for air and sealed my eyes.

The front bumper of the grey hatchback was a millisecond away from obliterating us.

Faster than a speeding bullet, Amir swerved to the other side, creating rolling clouds of smoke. Dear God, that was a close shave! The follicles on my head were ancient history.

"Am I alive?" I asked in a chipped voice. Amir leaned in and kissed me. After, he whispered, "In life, timing is everything."

We sailed away, and my curly hair spiraled into the shape of an orange traffic cone.

I prayed, *Dear God, can my hair blow like Mariah Carey's long, luscious locks in her music video, "Loverboy," where she rides on top of a speeding race-car wearing a double handkerchief bra that never blows away, and her tresses softly bounce in the gusty wind?*

Amir made one last turn on the highway, and the road merged into a brightly lit street that lead to a cul-de-sac where his parents lived in a home with three palm trees and a green lawn.

Hallelujah! I had arrived in one piece and miraculously with a full head of hair. But, we had one last bump in the road, literally!

Amir ran his car over a curb and parked it on the sidewalk in front of his parents' home because in Israel that is also considered private property. My head jerked back and forth and side to side from sudden impact.

He strolled out of the car, and I pushed my hair down because it had remained upward. I looked like I was done for.

He opened my door, and I dropped out of the car. That moment, I recalled "Loverboy" where Mariah Carey popped out of a cake undamaged.

Before he picked me up, Amir sang, "I'm clumsy and I know it," to the tune of LMFAO's song, "I'm sexy and I know it," because Amir firmly believed that I was as clumsy as a cow on roller skates.

Alas, I arrived at his parents' doorstep and tasted the sweet smell of freshly baked challah. Inside, I shook hands with a Persian Princess ("the Princess"), and my hands were as cold as ice. For the first time, the children sang the *berakhot* ("blessings" in Hebrew) over the red wine and challah in a New York minute. Everyone was eager to hear the Princess spill the (Persian) tea.

One could hear a pin drop. The Princess sat in the middle of the dinner table. I pondered, *What stories will she share? After all, discretion is the art of the geisha.*

Daphne served the Princess *fesenjoon* because she had guessed right that it was her favorite Persian stew.

Then, one of the children asked, "Are you a real Princess?" The Princess's face blushed by the unexpected compliment. I used my knife to push the fesenjoon and rice onto my fork and took a slow bite. My eyes stayed glued to the Princess, looking out for an answer.

Suddenly, I tasted Heaven! I wanted to scream, "MY OH MY OH MY!" a thousand times. But, *that* would take away from her spotlight.

Daphne had braised bone-in chicken thighs in a blend of toasted walnuts and pomegranate molasses. The sweet and sour flavors of the fesenjoon were out-of-this world! My tastebuds were piqued, and everyone was hypnotized by Daphne's fesenjoon. Right then, the Princess spilled the tea.

The Princess answered softly, "Yes, I'm a Persian princess." My eyes stayed glued. The Princess was a descendant of Ahmad Shah Qajar of Iran ("King Qajar"), and a tourist in Israel for the first time in her life. King Qajar was the King of Iran from 1909 to 1925.

My thoughts ran wild! Quickly, I collected myself and asked, "There were other Shahs before the legendary Pahlavi Dynasty?" She giggled and nodded, "Yes," and just like that, I forgot about Daphne's fesenjoon.

The Qajar dynasty had ruled Iran from 1794 to 1925, a whopping 131 years!

The children, enthralled, asked the Princess, "Do you live in a palace?" "Not quite," she answered graciously.

Suddenly, I realized that Amir had vanished. *This guy was slick but where did he go?* I thought.

The Princess took her first bite of Daphne's fesenjoon and sighed out loud, "This is divine." She sunk into her seat, slowly. The warm light from the Shabbat candles shined on her. I spotted deep lines around her brown eyes.

The children asked the Princess impatiently as they dipped challah in a cherry tomato dip, "Did King Qajar have spectacular birthday parties?" "Yes!" she exclaimed, surprisingly. King Qajar was only 11 years old when he ascended the throne!

How old is he now?" they asked tuned-in. "He would be very old," she said with a sweet grin.

Then, the children asked the Princess, "Did King Qajar live happily ever after?" The Princess somberly answered, "Not quite."

In 1923, King Qajar left Iran for Europe and seven years later, he died in exile. Upon his downfall, Reza Shah Pahlavi ceased the throne. In a wicked twist of fate, he and his son would meet the same fate as King Qajar.

The Princess, hopeful, said, "One can find light in the darkness." The children paused. She bashfully conjectured, "Isn't this the wisdom of Hanukkah?" Right then, it all had come full circle.

Many years ago, both of our families had lived in Iran and left to different places. In a serendipitous twist of fate, our paths crossed in Israel, an odd corner for a Persian princess.

Sudden waves of sadness *and* glory came rushing over me.

In the blink of an eye, Iran had lost its Jews and its last royal Persian dynasty. In the wake of the Revolution, tens of thousands of Persian Jews fled Iran and triumphantly returned to their ancestral homeland, Eretz Israel.

But can the Princess ever return to her homeland?

I felt a subtle brush against my shoulder, and Amir had returned. He glanced at me, puzzled by my pensive stare. He whispered in my ear with a serious tone, "We must leave." My body trembled from inside.

I panicked that he had suddenly been called to the front line. I glanced at the Princess and said, "Until next time, Your Royal Highness." She nodded her head in approval and said, *"Shalom and Khodâhâfez."* ("Khodâhâfez" is "goodbye" in Farsi.)

On our way out, I asked Amir, "Is it war?" He answered me with conviction and said, "No. If it was, you would never know that I had left."

The drive was slow and quiet, a pleasant surprise that kept me speechless. I pondered, *Where are we heading and why so sudden?*

He took side streets and back streets and sunken alleyways. *Alas, it's quiet,* I thought. In the still of the night, I remembered old stories which had escaped my mind.

On the night of my eldest brother's Bar-Mitzvah, my Dad had sat him down for a man-to-man talk. The guests had left. They reclined on two banquet chairs in the middle of the empty dance floor. The janitors swept the floors around them. The ceiling lights suddenly became brighter, putting a spotlight on them. A blue balloon had floated its way to my brother. "Leave it," my Dad told him in a serious tone.

"The day we left Iran, I went to say goodbye to my best friends," my Dad began.
"Who were they?" my brother asked tuned-in.
"They were my brothers," he said nostalgically.
"But, where they Jewish?" my brother asked inquisitively.
"No," my Dad said with a straight-face.
"Were you sad to say goodbye?" my brother asked him quietly.
"I came to their doorsteps in tears," my Dad said in a chipped voice.
"Did you ever get to say goodbye?" my brother asked curiously.
"They never opened their doors for me," my Dad answered with tears in his eyes.

Perhaps, my Dad's "best friends" believed deep-down that my Dad was an enemy. I wiped the tears from my eyes, and before I knew it, we had arrived at Jaffa, an ancient port city in South Tel Aviv.

Amir parked the car alongside the boardwalk and turned off the headlights without saying a word. The sky was clear and illuminated by bright stars.

The air was ice-cold and smelled like seawater from the ocean spray. I looked out and watched the waves crashing against the rocks that had been formed one on top of the other.

Softly, Amir took my hand and held it. He secretly put something in my palm. He asked me, "Does this belong to you?" I opened my hand and saw a ring.

The Wedding Singer

"Hotel California"

On July 7, 2017, I followed the whispers of my heart, and I married my romantic soulmate, Amir.

After I signed my *Ketubah* (Jewish Marriage Contract), I held my grandmother's hands, and I looked deep inside her tender eyes. I remembered her love story, and my heart travelled back in time to a kingdom far away from the seashores of sunny California.

Like Mother, Like Daughter

I was born in 1938 in the city of Rezaiyeh inside the Iranian province of Azerbajian.

I was 13 years old when I married my husband, Aaron, and he was 23. He is the love of my life and my best friend.

Every morning in Rezaiyeh, I would pass by his small wooden shop, and I would watch him sweep the stubborn dust that had settled at his storefront after nightfall. His hair was styled slick back, and he was dressed in a dapper dress shirt and tie. I cared for him, but I was too young to know "love."

Like mother, like daughter, my mom adored Aaron to her very last breath. Time after time, she prepared him *shefteh* (Persian meatballs). Once simmered, I took the reins to have the shefteh delivered to him fresh and unharmed by the heat of the Iranian sun.

One Thursday in 1952, I skillfully wrapped the burning pot with white terrycloth and secured the crown by tying a knot with a large loop. I gripped the loop and sped along the street market that was just waking up.

The steaming shefteh finally cooled down. Inside his shop, I unwrapped the pot and served him a feast on the same ceramic plate. I watched him take every bite with a big smile, and I waited for the moment when he got a gleam in his eyes that told me that he was in culinary euphoria.

The clock struck 8 o'clock, and I said goodbye. By then, the marketplace was buzzing. Flushed-face farmers bartered fresh hatched eggs, and fast-talking merchants sold sheepskin to survive Rezaiyeh's savage winter.

The aroma of fresh rustic bread treading air above the hustle and bustle was tantalizing. The baker spotted my hungry eyes, and it behooved me to accept his kind offer. Before long, a farmer's rooster grew noisy. He screamed "cock-a-doodle-do!" after each ringing beat of the tower clock bell, and his vibrating echos followed me like a marching band until I arrived at school.

After class, I played with my girlfriends outside of my home, and I saw Aaron's father arrive. My parents greeted him at our door, and they spoke inside. Moments later, he left and kissed me on my forehead.

The next day, I arrived at school with a slice of the baker's bread, and news was spreading like wildfire! My girlfriends teased me and said, "You're engaged!" I was clueless about the latest breaking gossip.

"I Wanna Hold Your Hand"

I received a surprise Saturday night when I heard a gentle knock on the door. Aaron stood behind the peephole dashing as ever. Like an arrow from a bow, my mom ushered me to my room. She dressed me in my favorite red dress that was embellished with white roses. After, she said, "Go with Aaron," and I followed her script.

I was on my very first date, and I didn't even know.

Aaron escorted me to his horse-drawn carriage (because there were no cars in Rezaiyeh), and the coachman boldly opened its door. The carriage was shaped like a pumpkin just like Cinderella's except mine was hinged with wood rather than gold.

The street market behaved differently at night-time. Peddlers ignited flavored tobacco through glass water pipes that erupted bubbles fighting for space inside the vessels. Plump old women cooked Turkish coffee in bronze ibriks over a tiny log fire that was protected by rocks and stones. Butchers showed off their prized meat when they grilled shish kebab on blazing *mangals* ("barbecue" in Farsi). The fragrant infusion of cinnamon, roasted Arabian beans, and charcoal swept through the hot air and found a resting spot inside our horse-drawn carriage.

Feeling bashful, I closed the lace curtains and exhaled a nervous smile. Even so, through the translucent lacework, I spied on the faces of hundreds that were hypnotized by the sudden extravaganza.

The crossroads leading to the cinema was more serene and delicate. The pavement was smooth, and entranced lovers held hands underneath the moonlight. Before then, I had never seen a movie on the silver screen.

Aaron chose middle row seats, and we watched an Indian romance. Somewhere between the star-crossed lovers locking eyes for the first time at a masquerade, and the envious debutante making her grand entrance on a purple elephant, Aaron gave me a kiss on the cheek. His tender kiss struck me like a bolt of lightning! Then, as he placed his hand over mine, I turned my palm around to hold his.

After the evil virgin fell to her death when she drank her own poison preceding the lovers' marriage, we took a stroll to the ice cream parlor. I chose the vanilla flavor because the chocolate had untimely melted away.

The next day, I was alone and heard the same gentle knock. When I opened the door, Aaron asked, "Are your parents home?" After I replied, he kissed my cheek and turned away. I watched the steady tempo of his footsteps, and I wondered when he would return.

That night, we went on our second date to the same Indian movie with Aaron's sisters and their husbands.

Their front row seats cost two Tomans courtesy of Aaron. Yet, he paid 15 Tomans for us to sit reclusively on red velvety chairs inside the balcony.

As the venomous landowner and his jealous niece framed the poor damsel of witchcraft only to keep the entangled lovers separated for eternity, I heard a loud scream. Ruben, Aaron's brother-in-law, jeered at him, "We sit economy, and you sit deluxe!"

The electrifying moment when the young man rescued his damsel in distress from the cruel icy barricades of the bent uncle's prison cell, I believed that the rumors at school were true. I was *also* happy to go to the movies and eat ice cream.

The Greatest Showman

The next Friday, Aaron ushered us into a stagecoach with a purpose and precision that I had always cherished.

I was thin and slightly shorter. Thus, I sat in between his two sisters and across from Aaron, who was long-legged and sat amid their husbands. When his feet reached mine, he liked to play footsie to steer my attention away from the gushing water well that came to be nothing but a mirage over hot gravel.

When we arrived at Lake Urmia, Aaron and I snuck away to the cherry fields. At first glance, the farmer forbade us to enter, and Aaron cajoled the one-eyed farmer to change his stubborn mind when he paid him two Tomans.

Aaron picked cherries, and I climbed up the tree to perch above the green grass that offered a bird's-eye view of the violet-and purple-colored fields. The bright red colored cherries seduced my tastebuds when Aaron reached up holding a bundle, and I diligently climbed down to meet him. We nestled underneath its branches and ate from the farmer's fruit basket.

Suddenly awakened by a wild rush of sugar that only Persian sweet cherries can ignite, we chased each other amid the complex maze of trees and hedges. After, I walked to the wood-fenced gate holding Aaron's hand, and the weary farmer finally returned to his cottage.

The tide was high while we slept on the beach. Faint whispers of tired seagulls flew over my head, and I tasted the salty water that had evaporated into the air. Yellow hills and white rocks surrounded our campsite and gave me a delightful sense of security. I imagined 1000 years ago when indigenous tribes would use the terrain as a fort against Genghis Khan.

Right after the Mongols fired their cannonball at the fortified village, I was awakened when I heard my name whispered. I saw a shadow on the sand, and just by the way that it held up my coat with two hands eager to sneak off once more, I knew that the shadow belonged to him.

The ominous beat that struck our hearts made by the leather sticks pounding against the tenor drums led Aaron and me to the carnival. Jugglers swung their raging torches 20 feet up into the black sky only to elegantly twirl down and land back into the palms of their hands. Their children pulled me into the dance circle and unable to coax Aaron to join the huddle, I caved in while he held onto my coat.

Onlookers, mostly Armenian, knew of Aaron's father because of his famous factory. They greeted their guest of honor with a host of berries, dates, nuts, and rich red wine. That night, I tasted the sweet future that would lie ahead for Aaron and me.

When the seagulls flocked west in a "V" shaped formation that was our cue to say goodbye. We returned without a trace before the sun rose, and like the flying birds, I glided back into my warm blanket undetected.

I pretended to sleep-in later than everyone else, and I blamed the bright sun for interrupting my dream.

I had butterflies in my stomach because tomorrow I had school. Aaron felt my nervous stomach after he looked into my eyes, and he prepared a honey cream sandwich to ease my trepidation.

The road to get back home seemed longer and felt rockier. Right when the front wheel of our one-horse carriage trampled over large stones, his sisters embraced me for dear life, and thus I was awakened by loud screams and tremors. Amidst our upheaval, the streets of Rezaiyeh were quietly asleep.

13 Going on 30

After school, I was too engrossed in deciphering the complex patterns of conjugating verbs from present to future tense to notice the army of frantic women barging into my parents' home. In unison, they screamed, "The army will draft *him*!"

Instantly and without an explanation, my mom dressed me in a brown dress and heavy coat because the clouds decided to snow that day. I was having déjà vu, only this time I perceived that the stakes were much higher. She steered me outside to a carriage packed with the same women who were by then out of breath.

I arrived alone to Aaron's sister's house and waited inside her dimly lit hallway. By then, it was nighttime, and the icy-cold streets also felt dark and threatening.

I saw the silhouettes of men and women entering the place where I waited. I knew when they walked past me by the brush of their coats against mine, and I would turn my head away.

They quizzed each other with the same question, "Have they brought the bride?" Their tone was inquisitive, yet denoted a sense of uneasy tension that maybe one shouldn't pose such anticipatory questions before the wedding contract has been signed and sealed. Still unsure that it was *my* wedding, I pondered, *Am I the bride?*

The guests wandered through the black-pitched hallway toward another entry. I caught a ray of light for a glimpse until the door rapidly closed behind them.

Moments later, a powerful hand wrapped itself around my wrist and pulled me toward the same door that had rapidly closed behind the guests. I walked with Aaron's sister into her bedroom.

Leading up to her boudoir, I struggled to make eye contact with their guests, hoping that one of them would be my parents. People were packed like sardines inside the living room, so the closely knit dynamics of it all made my mission impossible.

Aaron's mother handed me a long, white dress. While his sister fastened the back of my wedding gown by sliding pea-sized buttons into unyielding buttonholes, his mother grasped my elbow and kneeled.

Like the magician who woos his unassuming audience by pulling out the white rabbit inside his black hat from its ears, she too made safety pins appear from thin air. With all her speed and craft, she pinned the bottom of my dress inward to lift its length.

My ensemble was a plain, long sleeve satin gown with a round collar. The cream veil, made of lace, was tucked under my lily-white headband that cost three Tomans.

My father-in-law blessed me when he placed his hands on top of my head. In a state of shock, my mind was too busy to ask him, "Where is Aaron?"

Before I knew it, I stood alone in the middle of a densely populated living room encircled by jovial onlookers. Loud music was forbidden out of fear of attracting the army's attention, and so everyone overheard each other's careless whispers.

Behind my back, men began rooting for Aaron when they yelled in discord, "Throw the apples!" At the behest of tradition, Aaron tossed 100 hundred red apples, and anyone who caught them is believed to live a fruitful life.

I played competitively, and I walked outside to the garden bearing 11 apples. Our eyes met across the smokey hue that had arisen from grape stems that were being ignited in low flames. Aaron stretched out his arms to embrace me, as I lifted my dress and steadily walked across the fire to finally join him.

Magic illuminating from red sparks of fire cast a romantic spell upon us, and we forgot about time until we heard a heavy thumping. Aaron's father closed the garden door behind us to conceal the musical vibrations inside. A short, big, bellied man from the local cigar shop played his dombak and sang the same song. He chanted, *"Ay sheereen, Ay sheeren, Ay sheereeneh man!"* ("Oh sweetheart, Oh sweetheart, Oh my sweetheart of mine!").

I swirled in the middle of a chain dance when a man heckled, "A bride shouldn't dance so much!" I giggled at him in a cheeky manner that even caught me by surprise.

Meanwhile, old and portly women with aprons that were barely wrapped around their waists served meat on mix-matched ceramic dishes. After every bite, men quenched their thirst with rounds of shots drenched in homemade Russian style vodka, and the others whose palates were less parched sipped red wine.

Purple grapes that were plucked from the vines that were used for the fire, were served on tin trays as dessert, and that also signaled the final chapter of the night.

That evening, I slept in a room separate from Aaron since a new bride is considered a guest.

I was awakened at dawn by voices of young men shouting, "Take a bath!" Thinly dressed amid the freezing cold fog, Aaron leaped into a round wooden tub. When the batch of steam retired like a dozen drunken sailors, the same old and portly women could barely carry their pots, filled with boiled hot water to replenish his bath.

While he left to pray at synagogue, passersby threw shoes at his sister's front door. Upon Aaron's return, he tripped over a mountain of beat-up boots and heavy clogs.

The countless number of shoes symbolized the many children that he will father, and likewise he will stumble over their tiny moccasins and loafers. To make this prophecy come true, I greeted Aaron at the door shoeless.

Dressed in pink, I walked with Aaron to join his family inside his sister's living room. A long-bearded, holy man who called himself "Rabbi" ("the Rabbi"), sat between us on a wobbly bench. The sun's rays, emanating from the garden, gleamed on his face, which was covered with lines and spider veins. While we were the bride and groom, the Rabbi was always in the spotlight.

He served as a witness when Aaron and I signed the Ketubah that was made of lambskin and inscribed in Lishan Didan. My heartbeat raced a billion times the moment that Aaron paused to smile at me just before he stepped on glass. (In Jewish wedding ceremonies, the groom breaks glass to symbolize that happiness must always be tempered.)

Thereafter, the Rabbi rejoiced by shouting, "Mazel Tov!" and I was inducted as a married woman.

All along, my family stayed home because it was shameful for a bride's parents to be present.

Before long, they immigrated to Israel, and I saw them 13 years later with my four blessed children. When my father saw me for the first time, he said, "Your prophecy came true."

The Day a King Died

At 10:41 a.m. I read the headline. Confused, I turned to another television, and it read the same. It's even hard for me to write it: "Kobe Bryant, dead at 41."

My heart skipped many beats. The big restaurant quickly felt tiny. I dragged myself outside and *needed* to see my family. The air felt stale. On my way, a woman cried on the phone. "Kobe and his thirteen-year-old daughter, Gianna, died." I gave the sad woman a dirty look. *How dare she utter these evil words?*

I walked faster to ignore the vile chitter-chatter. I met my husband and baby breathless. I told him, "Kobe Bryant died."

To my dismay, he said, "Everyone dies."

My heart sank, and I felt too embarrassed to cry. I didn't *know* Kobe after all. So, I hid my sadness inside my heart.

My mind pictured Kobe embracing Gianna, the deafening sound of rotating propellers, screaming voices inside, wildfire and thick smoke, his wife, Vanessa's painful cries, and so much more. But still, no tears.

By coincidence, I had a therapy session the next day. I repeated to Dr. Q., "I'm so sad." He replied, "Yet, no tears. Why?"

I recall an Iranian boy crying for *lavashak* (persian style fruit leather). His mother yelled, *"Bacheh poru, geyreh nakon joloh mardom!"* Meaning, selfish child, don't cry in front of people.

I shared Kobe's story with my parents. My Dad said, "Don't talk about it, you will get sad." Unbeknownst to me, he was hurt.

Most Iranians were raised to believe that crying is shameful.

That morning, I was cold and wore a red sweater. As typical L.A. weather dictates, it became hot by 10 a.m. I left Dr. Q. stifled, and yet I kept my sweater. I was paralyzed with grief and remained still. Until suddenly, a wild rage of emotions roared inside me. I drove without end and cried for a *very* long time.

To me, Kobe was invincible, like the most powerful King in the world. So, how can a mighty and beloved King get killed?

Everything alive dies one day. This, is a fact of life.

I grappled with the *tragedy* behind Kobe Bryant's death.

He traveled in the Sikorsky S-7B helicopter with a reputation as stellar as its passengers.

I imagined Kobe rising from the burning smoke and heroically carrying Gianna.

Kobe was a member of my family. I proudly watched him flourish on and off the court.

Most of all, he was a devoted father. *Who will kiss his girls goodnight?*

The sheer enormity of Kobe's physical strength, unyielding power, and true grit did not save him.

Maybe, we really are everything and nothing.

One thing is absolute, Kobe Bryant taught me to embody self-compassion and to honor my dreams. He inspired me to practice every day, to never give up, and to play to win just like him.

Together, let us embrace compassion and savor every golden nugget in this precious reverie called "Life."

Don't Cry Because It's Over. Smile Because it Happened.
~ Dr. Seuss

Points of Reflection

Persian Tea is ideal for Middle School, High School, and University students.

The "Points of Reflection" is a teacher's guide to initiate meaningful conversation in the classroom and as topics for creative writing.

1. Why do you think Jasmine wrote this book?

2. Why do you think Jasmine chose this book title? If you could give the book a new title, what would it be?

3. Why do you think Jasmine chose to use movie titles for some of the chapters' titles?

4. Jasmine writes about how she believed that she was wanted by the FBI. Describe a time when you believed that your life or freedom was in jeopardy. Who was the antagonist and how did you survive?

5. Have you ever met a Persian Jew? What did/do you admire about him or her?

6. What positive contributions have immigrant groups and cultures given to America?

7. Jasmine writes about the story of Purim. Have you ever felt as an outsider? Describe what happened.

8. Which stories in your life would you chose to write about? What will you name your memoir and why?

9. There are examples of self-deprecating humor in Jasmine's stories. Why does she write about her painful experiences through humor rather than through drama? Does humor help you process painful times?

10. Do you ever laugh at yourself? To whom do you attribute your sense of humor?

11. There are stereotypes about Persian women. Do you think being funny is one of them?

12. Where is your family from? Share a unique custom from your country.

13. Did you or your parents immigrate to America and why? Who did you come with, and who did you leave behind?

14. Jasmine writes that Baba jan spoke Lishan Didan. Do you speak a "secret" language? What is your favorite expression?

15. Discuss this Hebrew quote: "Change your place, change your luck."

16. Which one of Jasmine's stories made you laugh out loud? Rewrite it without humor.

17. Have you travelled to Iran? What do you think it looks like?

18. Have you travelled to Israel? What do you think it looks like?

19. Jasmine writes that her Jewish parents fled Iran in 1979 because they feared genocide since one generation before them had lived during the Holocaust. (The "Holocaust" was the genocide of six million European Jews during World War II.)

The Federal Bureau of Investigation's 2020 hate crime statistics, released in 2021, showed that 54.9% of religious-bias hate crimes in America in 2020 targeted Jews. The Center for the Study of Hate and Extremism's 2023 Report to the Nation: Faith Under Fire, showed that 78% of religious-based hate crimes in major U.S. cities in 2022 targeted Jews. Yet, America's estimated 6.8 million Jews are only 2.1% of the nation's population.

Do you believe that Antisemitism exists in America and in the world today and why?

Do you believe that the world has learned from the mistakes of the past? Or rather, is history repeating itself?

Do you know what happened in Israel on October 7th, 2023?

20. Jasmine writes that she vaguely remembers her childhood. Do you believe that we intentionally forget about our past?

21. Jasmine writes about "taarof" in Persian culture. An example is: "You first please." Followed by, "No, after you." Then, back-and-forth until someone capitulates. Have you experienced Persian etiquette? Does your heritage have a similar cultural gesture?

22. Jasmine writes that she fell victim to the duplicity of other people. Yet, the Iranian Swissair Captain and Amos both saved her life. Do you believe that human nature is inherently evil or inherently good?

23. Jasmine writes that Michael Jackson's security guard was a "gigantic black bodyguard," and that she remained unafraid of him. Have you ever judged anyone by the color of their skin, height, and/or weight?

24. Jasmine writes that Amir is her soulmate. Do you believe in destiny or sheer luck?

25. Jasmine marries Amir who is Jewish like herself. Must two people must share the same culture and religion for a happy and lifelong marriage?

26. Jasmine writes about true love and her grandparents, and when her grandfather arrived in a horse-drawn carriage because there were no cars in Urmia. Has modern technology hindered romance and why?

27. Why did Jasmine write about Kobe Bryant? Who is your hero and why?

28. Jasmine writes about her father's bravery. What do you admire about him?

29. Do Jasmine's stories feel real to you?

Made in the USA
Las Vegas, NV
04 March 2024

86702758R00083